Dedication through Fasting and Prayer

by Nils-Erik Bergström

Nils-Erik Bergström
1102 Catlin Court
Simi Valley, CA 93065
USA
nils@enduringword.com

Dedication through Fasting and Prayer

by Nils-Erik Bergström

Table of Contents

DEDICATION THROUGH FASTING

DEDICATION THROUGH
BASIC LESSONS IN PERSONAL PRAYER

THE PURPOSE

This book was written for one reason: to equip the body of Christ, the Church - that means *you* - with the Word of God, and through faith to bring you to a lifestyle of more practical reasonable service. This can happen by the Holy Spirit's guidance working together with your yielding and dedication. Your mind and lifestyle will be delightfully transformed for God's purpose.

I want to encourage you to embrace this opportunity to actively engage in an everlasting, practical reasonable service through regular prayer and fasting, according to the teaching of our Lord. Jesus said in John 14:23, "All those who love Me will do what I say." This is really simply about dedication through love.

AN OPENING PRAYER

I thank my God and Father of our Lord Jesus Christ, that through the Holy Spirit's grace and guidance He has used me in presenting this book for His purpose. To Him be the praise and glory, because it is, in Him through Him and by Him, that His Word will do what He intends it to do in our individual life and in His body the Church now and forever, amen.

THANKS

A special word of gratitude to my Pastors - my son Yngve Bergström, and my son-in-law David Guzik. Without their help and encouragement this book would not have been possible.

Nils-Erik Bergström

START BY READING THIS

The Bible makes a difference between *practicing a dedicated pattern of life* through prayer and fasting regularly and doing it on *occasion*. This book will speak to both aspects so that we can be better equipped for our reasonable service to God and our fellow man. To follow the Word and to offer ourselves as a living sacrifice, we will focus on those two main objectives.

The first objective is that through the Holy Spirit's leading, to reveal what the Bible clearly teaches about fasting and prayer on a regular, weekly basis.

The second objective is to enable us - again, through the Holy Spirit's leading - what the Bible teaches about dedication through prayer and fasting on special occasions such as when our leaders ask us to do so, or when there are special needs to be addressed, or when the Holy Spirit leads us. We can be equipped to engage in yielding to God through fasting and prayer for longer periods, from three days up to 40 days.

The reason I repeatedly use the phrase "through the Holy Spirit's leading" is that we should not be led through man-made rules and regulations, but by the Spirit. The Spirit does not lead us to comply to the Law of Moses, but by the Spirit's leading and teaching we comply with a holy and dedicated lifestyle that does not contradict the Law of Moses. Therefore we are led by "Christ's Law" which is written in our heart. We don't have to wait until we feel led by the Spirit before we do what the Spirit tells us to do. We can start even if it feels like it is in the flesh, because we know from the Word of God that it is in the Spirit, no matter what our feelings tell us.

We can see the difference between Christ's law and Moses' law in that the Law of Moses was based on conditional prom-ises, so the motivation was to **do** in order to be blessed, or pay the consequences. The Law of Christ is based on the uncondi-tional New Covenant and so the motivation for obedience and devotion is different. Jesus Christ has paid the price already, we have been blessed and we are blessed, so therefore we **do**.

When we realize how God's people repeatedly humble themselves in this area of fasting - including Jesus - we should then learn this lesson about these two objectives, and to see the important emphasis the Spirit places on these issues. Do we consider ourselves above or behind in this area of devotion, or is it just a matter of ignorance or laziness? Certainly that time is past now and we will choose to yield to the truth, to be set free, to renew our thinking, to obey just like Jesus did, through the Holy Spirit's leading.

Introduction

Jesus said to the people, "I am the light of the world. If you follow me, you won't be stumbling through the darkness, because you will have the light that leads to life."
(John 8:12, New Living Translation)

Light leads to life. We want to bring out the light of God's Word regarding dedication through regular prayer and fasting and let it make a difference in our lifestyle. We want to do this to fulfill our personal calling and to glorify God's purpose for our life.

We are told to follow Jesus, and Jesus the Son of God fasted and taught us to fast. A former alcoholic or drug addict who has been set free from their habits is able to give a testimony to current alcoholics and drug addicts, and it has a great impact because they know what problems and difficulties they face. They speak their language.

In the same manner I give you my testimony as a former non-fasting Christian, because now I know what reasonable service means. I had missed that in my life, mostly through ignorance. I was not yielded or submitted in the area of prayer and fasting. I hope this book will help you receive and obey the truth as the Holy Spirit guides you, and that you will be delivered from ignorance in this area of dedication through prayer and fasting.

A common situation for an addicted person that wants to be set free is that they must first realize that they have a problem with their habits of living. Before they can be helped, they must want to be helped. Most of the time their reaction is to think, "*I can stop this at any time I like.*" This reaction will occur in an addict of any kind, and denying the problem only makes the addiction worse.

We know that being addicted to anything means to be ruled by that thing. We also know that this is really idolatry, and idolatry is nothing more or less than sin. When we put it this way, it's easy to see that we are all sinners.

I understand that we all like to defend our lifestyle. Perhaps you don't fit the picture of an addict. You think of yourself as a very ordinary person, free from drugs, alcohol, gambling, and other addictions. It's easy for you to say, "*I am a respected and good Christian, just as much as anyone else.*" That is absolutely true. But our problem might be that we are content to be just an "ordinary" or "regular" Christian.

The truth is that we are a new creation in Jesus Christ, and there is nothing ordinary in that. We are not to live like the rest of the world, not in any respect. We are chosen by God. Faith produces separation unto God, also through fasting and prayer. Faith that does not produce a constant change through the renewing of our mind is not a saving faith, and will not create growth.

When we do not deal with an addiction, an idolatry, or our regular and ordinary way of living, we do not mature at all and we cannot keep His works. Jesus told His Church in Revelation 3:15,

> *I know your works, that you are neither cold nor hot.*
> *I wish you were cold or hot.*

You may consider yourself dedicated, devoted and submitted, through your calling as a minister, pastor, priest or some other activity in your life - perhaps as a layperson through some involvement in the Church or some ministry. We can make ourselves so busy and occupied with these ministries and activities that we neglect basic matters of dedication to God like fasting and prayer.

Pursuing God in these other ways will contribute to your maturity, and then you will understand that dedication through fasting and prayer is Biblical, logical, and sensible. So let us take courage in the Word, and become more dedicated, devoted, humble and submitted for no other reason but for Him, our Lord Jesus Christ.

DEDICATION
THROUGH
FASTING

Part One
Does Devotion through Fasting Concern All Christians?

A Simple Answer to the Question

Of course devotion through regular fasting concerns all Christians, because *all godly direction concerns all God's children.* The only real issue is if we will *receive* and *obey* His direction, and if we will *adjust* our living according to God's direction. When His will is evident in us through the Holy Spirit's guidance, He will produce the fruit and then Christ-like character is plain to see. Isaiah 61:3 says, *For the LORD has planted them like strong and graceful oaks for His own glory.* An oak tree does not grow tall over a few years. Maturity takes time, living, and acting according to the Word in all areas of life, even in devotion through regular fasting.

The heart of him who has understanding seeks knowledge. (Proverbs 15:14) A long, godly persistent lifestyle will firmly establish a distinctively godly life.

Does God Direct Us to Devotion through Fasting?

Of course He does. There are 94 verses that mention fasting in the Bible, 46 in the New Testament and 48 in the Old Testament. As we take a look at some of those passages, I want to inspire you both through God's Word and my own experience. Since 1986 I have practiced reasonable service through fasting and prayer and I believe God has through His mercy and grace, taught me a lot about different aspects in life pertaining to this area of dedication, devotion, and submission through fasting.

Our faith is expressed in the habits of our life, not only by what we *say*. Faith without action is dead. When our lifestyle is based on the direction we receive from the Word of God, we will become godly. Consequently it will become difficult to ignore fasting in our devotion. Psalm 1:2 says of the godly,

But they delight in doing everything the LORD wants; day and night they think about his law. (Psalm 1:2, NLT)

If we apply this passage to the principle of devotional fasting, see that the godly *delight in doing everything the LORD wants* (including devotional fasting) and that *day and night* they meditate on His Word and think about ways to follow His guidance (even when it comes to fasting). Does our *delight in doing everything* God wants, actually include devotion through fasting? Of course it does. The word "delight" means a "high degree of gratification," also "extreme satisfaction, *something that gives great pleasure.*" Paul had something else to say about our *delight* in Romans 7:22:

For I delight in the law of God after the inward man.

If my delight is to obey, then my flesh must be in submission to the spirit - *the inward man.* Even though it is in the flesh that my action takes place, my guideline for obedience will come from the inward man, who should always be in charge.

The word *delight* shows that it isn't enough to simply *do* the will of God. No, we should do it delightfully. This means doing God's will with satisfaction, fulfillment, love, joy, peace, and a sense of well-being which follows obedience.

The pattern of our life will reflect our walk in the spirit, or our spirituality. Practical spirituality consists of the fruit of the Spirit as a vital part of our lifestyle. Therefore we make ourselves available to the Spirit for transformation. People may practice and work on showing some fruit, because anybody can show *some* patience or joy, or other aspects of the fruit of the Spirit. Even a non-Christian can show *some* kindness and gentleness.

But is the Holy Spirit at work producing them in their life? Galatians 5:22-23 describes the fruit of the Spirit:

But when the Holy Spirit controls our lives, he will produce this kind of fruit in us: love, joy, peace, patience, kindness, goodness, faithfulness, gentleness, and self-control. Here there is no conflict with the law. (Galatians 5:22-23, NLT)

When the Holy Spirit controls our life, He will produce this kind of fruit in us. So here there is no conflict with the law. The key the Holy Spirit's control, not our control. I am not implying that we are out of control. In that passage, Paul contrasts the fruit of the Spirit with the *works of the flesh*. It's clear that we aren't to think of the *works* of the Spirit, or of the *fruit* of the flesh.

Paul continued the idea in Galatians 5:24-25:

Those who belong to Christ Jesus have nailed the passions and desires of their sinful nature to his cross and crucified them there. If we are living now by the Holy Spirit, let us follow the Holy Spirit's leading in every part of our lives. (Galatians 5:24-25, NLT)

Every part of our lives certainly includes our passions and desires. Devotion through fasting promotes the Holy Spirit's leading in our life and the Holy Spirit will use our submission in this area of our life and so build our character.

A Common Situation

When our minds are set in preconceived judgments or opinions, or maybe confused or paralyzed by traditional views, we may see a truth in Scripture again and again and find that it never touches us, nor will it make an impression in our life to the point that it matters. It could be in any area of our life, but right now think of how many times you have read about fasting but have not let it become an issue in your life.

If you never have been exposed to this issue of how to offer service to God or man through dedication by fasting, this book will guide you to receive what the Word of God says about fasting. It will give fresh light regarding His intention for us when it comes to this particular area of service to God.

Many people excuse themselves from this reasonable service by saying, "I have other issues in my life that are more urgent to deal with before I devote myself to fasting. In fact I think that I need to 'fast' from some of my constantly repeatedly sin, before I engage in this godly service of fasting." Let me encourage you to understand that devotion through fasting will help you deal with these other issues. Perhaps devotion through fasting is just how God wants to help you to bring a breakthrough, a renewal, a different angle to your situation. What can you lose? You might only lose a couple of pounds, and any one of us can afford that. Charles G. Finney frequently used days of dedication through fasting and prayer in order to retain communion with God, because of his own weakness in the presence of temptation.

Keeping Balance

The time we live in is dominated by a love of selfish ease and comfortable affluence. So when we are exposed to Scriptures that speak to our need to deny our self, our easygoing lifestyle and attitude may be surprised by the seriousness and importance the Scripture emphasizes in this area.

Choosing rather to suffer affliction with the people of God than to enjoy the passing pleasures of sin. (Hebrews 11:25)

We might react sharply and make some drastic conclusions, that in turn could lead us to an unscriptural asceticism or legalism. This tendency lies dormant in our human nature, just waiting for the right condition to occur. When it does occur, it will show itself in zeal and pride, a sense of superiority, a kind of devotion, a false holiness if you will. This false spirituality is ready to show itself and rule over us, and to boast about our self-righteousness. This is the attitude and tendency that the hypocrites displayed, as Jesus pointed out again and again. John Wesley declared: "Some have exalted religious fasting beyond all Scripture and reason; and others have utterly disregarded it." We want to walk in the balance of God's Word.

The prevalent lifestyle of the world around us encourages us to pamper the flesh when we should buffet it. We as Christians should not be influenced by the world. Because we are a new creation we have our delight in completely different values that will show in the way that we live and conduct our self in all areas. To have a good time, to celebrate and to have a party together with friends and relatives has its place, of course. Just as much, devotional service to God or man through fasting has its place also.

There is a time to feast and have a good time, but fasting has its time also. A good time for a Christian can not be the same as what the world means with a good time. We are the ones to draw a clear line, and not indulge in the same manner as they do. We are not to participate and laugh at the same jokes and entertainment as they do, because we are free in Jesus Christ, and our joy is in Him.

There is nothing essentially vile or wrong with our human body. Because God our Father made our body, even with its desires and appetites. There is nothing evil in a hungry man's desire for a square meal, or a woman's longing for children and a home. The Holy Spirit is not teaching us to repress these normal instincts, but to control them and keep them within the bounds that the Bible prescribed, and ultimately to show them in a way that will glorify our Father in heaven.

The physical is not to be ruthlessly suppressed, but firmly disciplined and subordinated to the spiritual. The idea is to discipline my body, and make it obey through devotion by fasting.

*For the kingdom of God is not eating and drinking, but
righteousness and peace and joy in the Holy Spirit.*
(Romans 14:17)

Dwight L. Moody made the following statement: "If you say I will fast when God lays it on my heart, then you never will. You are cold and indifferent. Take the yoke upon you."

Part Two
How Do I Spiritually Prepare for Dedication through Fasting?

Holiness

To be dedicated and committed, and to do it delightfully for any cause will definitely show itself in our lifestyle. If our dedication and commitment to our God and Father does not characterize our behavior in everyday life, we must be careful about claiming that we really have faith in our God and Father.

Is it possible to separate our behavior and faith? No, that would be hypocritical. We know it is impossible to please God without faith, so we should beware of unbelief so that we do not fall away. This is a very serious statement from Hebrews, and what is even more interesting is to see that without holiness no one will see the Lord (Hebrews 12:14). There are many ways to be dedicated and committed, but when it comes to holiness it will take submission and dedication that affects our whole being, our entire lifestyle. That's why we will go step through step through dedication, submission, devotion, and yielding by the Holy Spirit's direction and by the way of reasonable service.

We Spiritually Dedicate through Fasting by Godly Living

Godly *direction* does not always lead to godly *living*. We understand that we have no problem listening and learning, but the problem starts when we begin to apply the truth to our life situation. We often have trouble finding time to read the Bible, but a book on any other subject we often find time for. I know what this was like in my own life.

Faith is an activity in all three parts of our created being: body, soul, and spirit. Faith is spiritual, practical, affectionate, and passionate. Without faith we can not please God, the Father of our Lord Jesus. Faith without works is dead, as mentioned three times in the second chapter of James. There is no eternal life or salvation without present eternal living or active faith, coming through our belief in Jesus and the conversion of our heart. Then out of love we will act according to His Word.

We Spiritually Dedicate through Fasting by Understanding what Reasonable Service Means

We know that God's will for our life is good and right, even to the point of perfection. He looks at His will for our life with great pleasure. Knowing this about God's will makes us long to achieve it in our life. When His will becomes real in our life our life is in tune with the leading of the Holy Spirit. When our whole being is occupied with our longing to please Jesus who is the Way, the Truth, and the Life - the Way to be walked, the Truth to be used, and the Life to be lived - then we can be assured that we are on our way to salvation. We delight in doing everything God wants us to do because then we become like He is, holy and obedient.

Dedication through fasting will sustain us in this effort. This is because dedication through fasting is what God wants for us, and He knows what is best for us. He will even reward us openly when we do it for the right reason and in accord with His Word. To be completely dedicated through fasting with the right perspective, we must believe and be totally persuaded that it is God's will for our life, and as a child of God I must adjust the pattern of my life according to His Word.

Submission through regular fasting and prayer doesn't only

mean to stop eating and to only pray. We must also be prepared to renew our mind, to be ready to think differently. The submission that comes through fasting will change us, but not in a way that reminds us of this world's standard. This is a good rule, regardless of what area we work with in our life. When we look closer in the Word of God we find that it is not only a rule but a very urgent appeal through the Apostle Paul by the mercies of God:

I beseech you therefore, brethren, by the mercies of God, that you present your bodies a living sacrifice, holy, acceptable unto God, which is your reasonable service.
(Romans 12:1)

Reasonable service is explained in several words, such as:

- To be within reason
- Not asking too much
- Logical
- Sensible
- Sound
- Restrained
- Not to extremes
- Controlled
- Moderate

Can it be that these nine descriptions of *reasonable service* also describe dedication through fasting? Yes, they do. Is the Bible that plain? Of course, the Scripture does speak this clearly to us about dedication through fasting. To *present our bodies* means simply:

- To give of our self
- To offer our self
- To be available
- To be a living sacrifice, holy and acceptable to God

Fasting is one important way to present our bodies. It calls for a total involvement, but it is involvement *in Christ*, because we will become holy through Christ by letting the Holy Spirit change us. According to Martin Luther, "Each one of us is in himself a Devil, but in Christ we are saints." According to what the Apostle Paul wrote, all that takes place in us should be according to God's will. Then we must understand how to change our lifestyle and that reality lays in allowing our mind to be renewed, as explained in the next verse, Romans 12:2:

Don't copy the behavior and customs of this world, but let God transform you into a new person by changing the way you think. Then you will know what God wants you to do, and you will know how good and pleasing and perfect his will really is. (Romans 12:2, NLT)

When His will is that we give our self to devoted service by fasting then that is good, pleasing, and perfect. *Transform* implies a major change, a change in character or condition. One of the synonyms for the word *transform* is *convert*, which implies a change fitting something for a new or different use or function. Yes, we have to start to function according to the Word of God, and do it by submitted service through fasting regularly.

Do we dare to change our way of thinking? Yes! It can happen as we let God transform us. According to our new way of thinking we become obligated to act in a new way. As we realize and practice the renewal of our mind, we will be certain and overwhelmingly sure what the perfect will of God is. Because the Holy Spirit lives in us and lives in our mind, so it is God's work in us when we renew our mind according to His will. Remember that we are focusing on the idea of renewing our mind as it applies to the area of dedication through fasting regularly.

Therefore, it is impossible to go on living the way we do. Renewal must take place. A permanent change can only take place when we renew our mind constantly. Is that possible? Of course it is possible through Christ who dwells in us by faith. How exceedingly strong is the power is that works in us if we choose to make it work in our everyday life by yielding to Him. When we let God enable us, we surrender and give up our own selfish thinking.

Be diligent to present yourself approved to God, a worker who does not need to be ashamed, rightly dividing the word of truth. (2 Timothy 2:15)

To present yourself approved means more than just listening to teaching. It also means *rightly dividing the truth*. That is why we prepare to renew our minds so that we can become transformed to rightly divide the word of truth ourselves.

Are we *transformed*? Are we *different*?

Martin Luther wrote: "A Christian should be a new creation, or one of God's new created beings, that in most of his life, talking, thinking, and judging differently than what the people of the world do." Therefore, as Christians we act differently, not like others. This even includes not having the same eating habits as those who are of this world, or the same eating habits as those Christians who don't submit to the teaching of Jesus by devotion through fasting but instead live a lifestyle like the world does.

We can summarize these ideas with Ephesians 4:22-24:

Throw off your old evil nature and your former way of life, which is rotten through and through, full of lust and deception. Instead, there must be a spiritual renewal of your thoughts and attitudes. You must display a new nature because you are a new person, created in God's likeness - righteous, holy, and true.

These are good words, without any legalistic pressure or condemnation. It is clear that we must *display* - that means to show in our lives - obedience, just like Jesus did.

Though He was a Son, yet He learned obedience.
(Hebrews 5:8)

We Spiritually Dedicate through Fasting by Receiving Correction, Approval, and Instruction

We need all three of these tools to teach us about dedication through fasting regularly. When we turn to Him for guidance, we have good reason to expect these three tools to meet and help us. It is right to expect that God's Word will equip us and make us ready for all actions motivated by our love for our Father and God of our Lord Jesus Christ, and His Word will equip us for a dedicated yielded spirit to fast and pray.

> *All Scripture is inspired by God and is useful to teach us what is true and to make us realize what is wrong in our lives.* (2 Timothy 3:16, NLT)

- The Word of God straightens us out
- The Word of God teaches us
- The Word of God guides us to do what is right

The Word of God discerns the thoughts and intents of the heart and is full of living power and it will clearly point out what is wrong in our life. It directs and teaches us to do the right thing. Then our part is to act according to the Word of God, to obediently follow that direction, in whatever area in our life that might be. At this moment, we focus on the direction God's Word gives us regarding submission through fasting. God uses His Word to prepare us in every way - including submission - to make us fully equipped for every good thing God wants us to do, to make us ready for every loving action, to become a godly and mature person.

We have reached a good goal when we practically know how to change our mind, to do and become different for the sake of becoming dedicated and holy because we love Him, our Lord. If we have a problem as we endeavor to reach that goal, let us look again at the reason for that. When we carry preconceived thoughts and opinions that are conditioned by our mind the result is that we are occupied or possessed - even somewhat paralyzed - with worldly inspired traditional views. So we face a truth in Scripture again and again without it doing anything in our life and we are untouched. We act as if it doesn't matter.

Our spiritual inhibition or restriction concerning the truth makes us to trip - to make a mistake or a false step - with three P's:

- **Permits** us to see the truth
- But not to **Perceive** the truth
- Or to **Pursue**, to carry the truth out in action

This is particularly true in relation to dedication, devotion, and submission through fasting. With what I write I am not trying to persuade you to fast or to renew your mind - I can't make anyone do anything - but I know someone Who is able! You know Him too - the Helper, the Holy Spirit, whom the Father will send in Jesus' name, is more than able to make these principles alive in this area of dedication, devotion and submission through fasting regularly.

When He makes such a truth come alive in your spirit, there immediately rises a conflict in the minds of the people that I just described. The truth has suddenly become "alive and powerful" and there is an assault upon our traditional attitudes, values, opinions, and the flesh will not submit willingly. Our attitude may stand against what God's Word and the Holy Spirit tells us to do. The outcome of that struggle will reveal whether or not we are open to receive and obey such truth and grow in the knowledge of what God intends for us when it (1) concerns reasonable service through fasting as a consistent practice and (2) concerns fasting on special occasions.

We must make practical changes in our lifestyle - creating time and place in our schedule - so that we can receive the Word in a consistent, personal way, to act in a way that the result will make a real impact on our life. It may even reach the point of rearranging our lives in order to be obedient when the Holy

Spirit is leading. Yielding by fasting regularly is a good start in that direction.

Dedication through fasting or some other disciplined lifestyle is not the *goal* but the *way* to achieve the result, because when it comes to the Spirit's moving in us it is up to Him. Submission is well fitting here, yes to make our self obedient, available, ready, and willing.

Proverbs 3:5 says, *Trust in the* L<small>ORD</small> *with all your heart, and lean not on your own understanding.* This means that our own ideas are no longer needed. Proverbs 3:5 continues, *In all your ways acknowledge Him, and He shall direct your paths.* This means that you are not to create any of your own solutions or patterns.

An old saying tells us that good intentions pave the road to hell. We must go beyond our good intentions and *wishing* things were different in our spiritual lives. To go beyond mere good intentions, we must do our part. To fulfill our part we must have our life guided by His Word. When our hearts are flooded by the power of our dedication, that will show forth in humble, obedient, and affectionate devotion. We will delightfully act out the Word our heart is saturated with as an everyday lifestyle.

It is not that we think we can do anything of lasting value by ourselves. Our only power and success come from God. He is the one who has enabled us to represent his new covenant. This is a covenant, not of written laws, but of the Spirit. The old way ends in death; in the new way, the Holy Spirit gives life. (2 Corinthians 3:5, NLT)

It is worth repeating, that in our relationship with our Father, it is the power through the Word - Jesus Christ - that penetrates our heart as we read in Ephesians 1:19-20:

And what is the exceeding greatness of His power toward us who believe, according to the working of His mighty power (that same power) *which He worked in Christ when He raised Him from the dead and seated Him at His right hand in the heavenly places.*

We who believe and have the assurance faith brings will see faith continue to grow through the Word that we take in, on an everyday basis. As we act on the Word, it gives life and power.

A good motivation to do something is not the same as renewing our mind! The transforming power happens when we renew our mind, and it creates a situation allowing the new principle for our behavior to become real in our everyday lifestyle, as the changes take place.

Again I think it is worth repeating that we do not fast for the sake of simply doing it. Instead it is a matter of what the Word does in us. Our response to His Word is what matters. As we present our bodies we make our life available for what the Word does in our heart, and then we are ready to act.

Because the Word is sharper than any two-edged sword, it will separate the soul and the spirit. Our mind, the way we think, will be transformed when the Spirit gains our full attention, and we respond in wanting to bless our loving Father with our surrender, obedience, and devotion. Our whole mental attitude has to be radically renewed again and again. We could even use the terms "revived" or "changed in our inner man," or to be "filled with the Holy Spirit." Now, if we have been able to comprehend and rightly understand how to practically adopt this teaching about how to renew our minds according to the will of God, it will be a great advantage to apply that to the teaching about dedication through prayer and fasting. In fact, this is an exceedingly excellent way.

You probably understand by now that dedication through fasting will have a deeper impact on your life than you thought, but it has to do with your conviction that it is *God's direction for your life* and your *obedient humble response* to submit.

Preparing Our Minds and Hearts for Devotion through Fasting

Before we look at some chosen Bible passages regarding this subject, let us spend some time to be cleansed and released from all knowledge and understanding that we have accumulated that is not based on the Bible. We get so much input from sources that aren't inspired by God. Articles in magazines, books, and newspapers. Radio programs, television, school, home, friends, or relatives that aren't influenced by the Word, regardless if we are aware of it or not. Even a popular Bible handbook emphasizes the importance of Bible reading but states, "that there are occasions when fasting is proper, but that it is out of place in an ordinary life." Such ignorance is surprising. No wonder devotion through fasting is so neglected and unknown, when people pay attention to such unbiblical teaching. This is why I believe that we should let the Bible explain itself and let Scripture explain and reveal Scripture.

A well known leader in the church made a comment not long ago - I heard it myself - he said that fasting is almost impossible for a normal Christian who has to go to work every day or be a homemaker. He excluded the idea of fasting for any length of time, and absolutely thought that someone should not - or could not - fast regularly. He said that he had a hard time making it through a whole day of fasting himself. This is misleading nonsense.

A doctor, pastor, or church leader who thinks and teaches wrongly in this subject may anyhow be used of God. But he makes a mistake with such remarks, and I can definitely say he is wrong in these areas and oppose his words as being false. Our understanding of the Bible and our personal experience tells us differently.

Jesus believed we could live our everyday life and still fast regularly. In fact, Jesus said that when we fast, "Do not appear to men to be fasting." The idea is that we should go on our daily routine as usual. In my own experience, I have gone for 14 days without food, drinking only water the entire time, while every day working hard for 10 to 12 hours and I did not find it difficult. I have no reason to over-emphasize my experience. This book is not only based on my experience, but on the Word of God and my testimony is about how the Word has directed my lifestyle through His grace.

Even though this pastor did not establish any rule that people should not fast, he certainly harmed the body in the area of understanding dedication through fasting by his teaching. No wonder dedication through fasting is so neglected.

It is important to know that dedication through fasting for the sake of only fasting, just to be in charge of our will as a religious, self-imposed act, is of no value whatsoever. When you allow yourself to experience what the Bible actually teaches on this subject you will practice reasonable service on a regular basis and become more like Him, our Teacher, Jesus Christ.

Remember this principle from the Holy Spirit through the Apostle Paul:

These rules may seem wise because they require strong devotion, humility, and severe bodily discipline. But they have no effect when it comes to conquering a person's evil thoughts and desires. (Colossians 2:23, NLT)

Understanding the Word "Fast"

Let us establish that the word "fast" means only one thing: to simply not eat, to hold one's self off, to keep one's self from, to abstain from solid or liquid food or nourishment of any kind. When I speak of fasting, I mean to do this for a set period of 24 hours or more.

Does everybody understand this definition of fasting? Not necessarily. The fact remains there are many forms of so-called fasting that are practiced in the Christian community today, allowing any kind of fruit or vegetable juice, protein drinks, milk, and so forth.

There are three kinds of fasting described in the Bible.

First there is the "normal fast," which is abstaining from all kinds of foods and drinking only water. This is the kind of fast Jesus did in Matthew 4:2.

Second is the "absolute fast" which is to abstain from both food and water, referred to in Acts 9:9 and Esther 4:16 where it explicitly is written *"neither eat nor drink for three days, night or day."* To this category we add Moses' 40 day fast in Exodus 34:28, and Elijah's fast in 1 Kings 19:8, but those fasts were supernatural. We understand they were only possible through a supernatural intervention from God.

The third is the "partial fast" described in one passage, Daniel 10:2 and 3:

When this vision came to me, I, Daniel, had been in mourning for three weeks. All that time I had eaten no rich food or meat, had drunk no wine, and had used no fragrant oils.

However, this passage from Daniel does not even use the word "fasting." We might even say that this isn't Biblical fasting, just another form of denying self. Remember that the terms "normal fast," "absolute fast," and "partial fast" are not Biblical, but just names that are commonly used to describe what we find in these Bible passages.

Some people think that you can just skip one meal or simply abstain from meat for a day and still call it fasting. The proper name for that is "dieting," not fasting. Some people associate different names with different types of fasting, such as the "John the Baptist Fast," the "Saint Paul Fast," the "Widow's Fast," the "Elijah Fast," the "Samuel Fast" and on and on. But this expands the meaning of "fasting" so much that the word doesn't have much meaning any more. If anything relating to food or eating can be called fasting, then we have no need for what the Bible says about fasting. There is nothing wrong with dieting, but the word "fast" means to totally abstain from all kinds of nourishment, solid or liquid except for water, and to do it for a set period of time, usually 24 hours or more.

It is so easy to get off the simple truth of God's Word and be deceived. Take a look at other areas that have affected the church, such as baptism, worship, ordination, baptism in the

Holy Spirit, the gifts of the Spirit and so forth. If we only could stick to the Word of God and let it explain and interpret itself!

Understanding the Word "Fast" Mentally and with the Right Attitude

Again I like to emphasize when I use the word "fast," some can practice it as an act in itself, without any connection to the real *intention*. Then it becomes just a form, and is in itself only a ritual. Like prayer is communication and consists of words, if we say the words without heart or meaning the prayer becomes just a ritual. So when I use the word "fasting," remember that is has to do with dedicated, devoted submission to God that results in practical, reasonable service, first to God and secondly to man. I will continually emphasize this issue throughout the book.

If we pray often, does it build our faith? Yes, but it depends on *how* we pray. When Jesus was asked to teach on prayer, He continued to teach on fasting also, as if those two areas belonged together. Consequently the same goes for fasting. If we fast often it builds our faith by the same principle, it will depend on *how* we fast. There is no need for us to make fasting complicated, or make a new doctrine to hang our hat on. If we are serious about maturity we have to do things according to God's Word or we will end up worse than when we started.

If you have pursued fasting and haven't made any progress, it is possible that some of your man-made *attitudes* should go. Take a stand and make a decision, let go of the old, to let go of your ignorance, and to become free. We will be sanctified and cleansed by the washing through the Word, Jesus Christ.

The goal of our life is not to gain maturity through being obedient by fasting and prayer. Our goal should be a heart-felt desire to obey God, according to the Holy Spirit's leading. Maturity describes someone who has their senses trained through dedicated, submitted devotion to God out of a humble and repentant heart. Then obedience through fasting follows.

But God be thanked that though you were slaves of sin, yet you obeyed from the heart that form of doctrine to which you were delivered. And having been set free from sin, you became slaves of righteousness. (Romans 6:17-18)

Not with eyeservice, as men-pleasures, but as bondservants of Christ, doing the will of God from the heart. (Ephesians 6:6)

Obedience is an Act of Love

Here are a few things I have learned about obedience, especially as it relates to submission through fasting.

1. Obedience releases submission, which is the thankful response in the heart of those who receive deliverance and freedom in Christ.

2. Obedience is practically lived in a holy and mature lifestyle, becoming a submitted servant to the calling and claim through God's will placed in our heart through the revelation of the Word.

3. Here are two passages of Scripture that tell us much about obedience:

Love has been perfected among us in this: that we may have boldness in the day of judgment; because as He is, so are we in this world. (1 John 4:17)

And everyone who has this hope in Him purifies himself, just as He is pure. (1 John 3:3)

This means that love is perfected in boldness, because obedience and purification are connected to being like He is. That's easy to understand, but doing it takes love.

4. Another important passage of Scripture is 2 Corinthians 10:5-6:

Casting down arguments and every high thing that exalts itself against the knowledge of God, bringing every thought into captivity to the obedience of Christ, and being ready to punish all disobedience when your obedience is fulfilled.

The idea is that we realize His love and what He wants for us. Then come other thoughts that contradict and delay our ability to believe and act in faith. We immediately have to deal with those thoughts, and renew our mind. Our mind is the battlefield, so we must carry out the punishment against those thoughts severely. How do we punish a thought? By eliminating it from our mind before it creates something bad. Let us do just that!

Let us pray using the ideas from 2 Corinthians 10:3-5:

"Even though I am an ordinary regular person, when I do warfare I do not do it like regular people do, because I do it in the spirit, in my newly created man in God, through dedicated prayer right now. Father I thank You for Your guidance. I am strong in You. I know what keeps me from victory; yes, yes, I know the stronghold in my mind, I do tear it down and cast it out, right now because it does not make me submitted to Christ. Amen."

Let us continue to pray by using most of the words from Psalm 119:12-18 (NLT). I have added the words in the parenthesis to relate this passage to the idea of dedication through fasting.

Blessed are you, O LORD; teach me your principles. I will study your commandments and reflect on your ways, I will delight in your principles and not forget your word, be good to (me) *your servant, that I may live and obey your word, open my eyes to see the wonderful truths in your law* (about dedication and submission to reasonable service through fasting and prayer).

As the Apostle Paul puts it in Philippians 3:13: "Forgetting those things that which are behind and reaching forward to those things which are ahead."

Part Three
Who Should Fast?

Who Should Fast?

It's good to consider the *who*, the *why*, and the *how* when it comes to devotion, dedication, and submission through fasting. So let us get started with the question, "*Who* - who should be involved in fasting?"

Deuteronomy 8:3 (NLT) speaks to this point:

Yes, he humbled you by letting you go hungry and then feeding you with manna, a food previously unknown to you and your ancestors. He did it to teach you that people need more than bread for their life; real life comes by feeding on every word of the LORD.

Please, take a look at this phrase: "He did it to teach you, by your hunger." Let us prepare to pursue this teaching. Notice that we must get hungry in order to be taught. This means that real life and nourishment comes by feeding on every word that comes from our God and Father. Are you prepared to accept that teaching?

That is from the Old Covenant. Let us find the same principle in the New Covenant, when Jesus uses the same words in Matthew 4:3-4:

After that He had fasted for 40 days and 40 nights. Now when the tempter came to Him, he said, "If You are the Son of God, command that these stones become bread." But He answered and said, "It is written, 'Man shall not live by bread alone, but by every word that proceeds from the mouth of God.'"

So God speaks to mankind, to His creation, and His Word is

for you and me. Who should go hungry and not live by bread alone? That question is easily answered. Every one of us should learn to go hungry and live by more than bread alone, not only the clergy or "special" Christians.

When the disciples discovered that Jesus was not eating, we should understand that He yielded through fasting without the disciples' knowledge. In this, Jesus simply did what He taught. We will come back to that later, but this is how Jesus replied in John 4:32-34:

But He said to them, "I have food to eat of which you do not know." Therefore the disciples said to one another, "Has anyone brought Him anything to eat?" Jesus said to them, "My food is to do the will of Him who sent Me, and to finish His work."

Have you been so busy that you forgot to eat or so occupied that you were not hungry? Or have you ever just plain forgot about food? Jesus was so consumed with doing the will of His Father that fasting became part of His lifestyle. It showed that He did not live by bread alone.

Jesus Teaches About Fasting

In Matthew 6:5-18, Jesus taught about prayer and fasting, and He starts in Matthew 6:5 with "when you pray . . ." Jesus continued in Matthew 6:16 saying, "when you fast." The question is not *if* you should fast, as the statement of Jesus reveals. He takes it for granted that they *are* fasting and *will* fast. I will not deal with the argument that it was part of *their* culture, and it is not part of *our* culture. There are many books written about prayer but only a few of them about fasting, even though these two aspects belong together. Fasting certainly isn't a habit in our culture, nor is it a common teaching in our Churches. Why should it be like this when it makes such a difference?

If we accept that the prayer Jesus taught the disciples concerns us, then His teaching about fasting also concerns us and belongs to us.

That conclusion is obvious and we can understand that fasting must be part of our lifestyle just as prayer should be. This concerns me as a child of God, as a disciple of Christ, and as a mature Christian, who wants to be in the will of God in all areas of devotion, including both prayer and fasting on a regular basis.

Another place where Jesus is clear to the point is where He states "they *will* fast" in Matthew 9:14 and 15:

Then the disciples of John came to Him, saying, "Why do we and the Pharisees fast often, but Your disciples do not fast?" And Jesus said to them, "Can the friends of the bridegroom mourn as long as the bridegroom is with them? But the days will come when the bridegroom will be taken away from them, and then they will fast."

If Jesus assumed that His disciples would fast, it certainly goes for us also. So, who should fast? We all should fast, of course!

These passages from the Scripture give us assurance regarding *who* should fast, and that fasting belongs to all Christians. The first Church practiced fasting on a continuous basis as a part of their lifestyle and service to God and men:

As they ministered to the Lord and fasted, then, having fasted and prayed, and laid hands on them, they sent them away. (Acts 13:2)

So Cornelius said, "Four days ago I was fasting until this hour." (Acts 10:30)

We may learn from a man of God like Charles G. Finney, who wrote: "I often feel myself weak in the presence of temptation and needed frequently to hold days of fasting and prayer and to spend much time in overhauling my own religious life in order to retain that communion with God." I like the way he expressed what fasting does: "to retain that communion."

Part Four
Why Should We Fast?

Why Should We Fast?

Martin Luther made a very good and pointed answer to this question. "One should not be fasting in order to do a good deed, but only and I mean only in order to be equipped and fitted to live in accordance with the Word of God." Which of us does not have that goal in our life? We all want to be prepared for service and close to God according to the Word of God. To submit through fasting might be a new approach and seemingly not often used, but I want to encourage you to let the Word lead you, and then to yield yourself.

In advocating fasting as a lifestyle, I get different responses from Christians from all kinds of backgrounds, even from people who seem to have a good understanding of the Bible. Most of us like to defend our non-Biblical lifestyle in whatever area we are confronted with. Some of the excuses for not fasting I have heard from these people are:

- "I never noticed the importance of fasting though I have read through the Bible 16 times"
- "Love is more important than fasting"
- "God never spoke to me about fasting"
- "That sounds so legalistic"

The word "legalistic" means: "to not have a free choice, strict, excessive conformity to the law, or to a religious moral code." Therefore, legalism *restricts free choice*. I understand that legalism on one hand and lukewarm faith on the other hand are two extremes and both are traps that we should avoid. The enemy does not care which ditch we fall into as long as we are not dynamic shining lights. Ignorance does not belong to us in

41

any area of our life.

Yielding through fasting is only one part of our behavior as a Christian, but it is an important part that often is neglected because we think it is so difficult. Remember it is not difficult when your heart is convinced. Many of us know what it is to develop other areas of our Christian behavior like individual time for prayer, Bible study, or praise and worship. We may know the need to set time aside for to meditate and fellowship with our Father and God. All those different activities are *made better* through dedicated fasting - believe me, I know that.

All those different activities are marks of mature Christians who have their senses exercised, who display a living faith in accord with the Word and the Spirit's devotion. Yielding through fasting not only benefits us in all those areas, we will also be rewarded. Notice, I am not stating that fasting alone is the mark of a mature Christian.

So why should we fast? First of all, devotion through fasting belongs to our service, our ministry before our Father according to Acts 13:2-3. Secondly, it belongs to our service, our ministry to other men.

As they ministered to the Lord and fasted, the Holy Spirit said, "Now separate to Me Barnabas and Saul for the work to which I have called them." Then, having fasted and prayed, and laid hands on them, they sent them away.
(Acts 13:2)

In the church certain prophets and teachers ministered to the Lord. The majority of church leaders and congregations today neglect this aspect of church life and they do not practice yielding through fasting as an aspect of ministry. Yet in the divine order ministry to the Lord comes before ministry to men. As a consequence of ministering to the Lord, the Holy Spirit brings forth the direction and the power through grace needed for effective ministry to men.

Please, follow this carefully. Take a look in Acts 13:2 and see how the direction was given. It came while they *ministered to the Lord and fasted.* That was the first occasion. But after looking at Acts 13:3 we see that there is more to it than that. Acts 13:3 describes how they fasted a second time, because they needed the gift of the special grace and direction necessary for the task that lay ahead.

To have a prayer meeting as a breakfast or lunch gathering is a common thing nowadays. Please, don't get offended. If that will make people come out, there is not anything wrong with that, but do you see that it just emphasizes the fact that our lifestyle usually does not include fasting. Even prayer meetings have become eating occasions, as is a common practice in our churches, as well as in our individual life. When it comes to dedication services and the appointment of elders and so on, we can read about it in Acts 14:23:

So when they had appointed elders in every church, and prayed with fasting, they commended them to the Lord in whom they had believed.

In the early church it became a pattern. As they were taught, they in turn taught others.

We allow our selves to be limited, and there are some services that we are not able to perform without prayer and fasting, as Jesus said in Mark 9:14-29. This is a passage you probably are familiar with. As we look at it again, notice that there is no substitute for the way it says to do these things.

And when He had come into the house, His disciples asked Him privately, "Why could we not cast it out?" So He said to them, "This kind can come out by nothing but prayer and fasting." (Mark 9:28-29)

It is important to acknowledge regularly that dedication through fasting is a tool to meet the special needs in our ministries, in individuals, and in our congregations. If we don't, then our attitude will become negligent, and we don't function according to the Word of God. Instead we expose ourselves to mistrust and risk becoming unfaithful. But not any longer.

Maturity Versus Obedience

If for some reason you are not mature enough to decide that dedication through fasting should become a part of your lifestyle according to the Word of God, you may be encouraged to understand that maturity sometimes *follows* obedience. Let us encourage each other to make the most of the possibilities reasonable service through fasting promises, to draw near to Him, our teacher of fasting and prayer Jesus Christ, who is our head-shepherd and Master. Obedience is not earned, but it is learned, and so is maturity. Positively will we from now on, diligently learn just that "obedience."

You go, therefore, and read from the scroll which you have written at my instruction, the words of the LORD, in the hearing of the people in the Lord's house on the day of fasting. And you shall also read them in the hearing of all Judah who come from their cities. (Jeremiah 36:6)

On the Day of Fasting

Should we be part of the body of Christ and act according to His direction and His example?

If the answer is "Yes" then fasting will be part of our natural way of life, our belief, our devotion, and our life in Him. Fasting is part of what it means to present our members as slaves of righteousness and holiness. This means that I, as a part of the body, will bring edification to the rest of the body, our Church.

The goal of our life is not to gain maturity trough fasting or by being obedient to the written Word of God. The goal is that our life should be directed from our heart's desire to obey, according to the Holy Spirit's leading. We should have a heart to do this to the benefit of the whole body.

But God be thanked that though you were slaves of sin, yet you obeyed from the heart that form of doctrine to which you

*were delivered. And having been set free from sin, you be-
came slaves of righteousness.* (Romans 6:17-18)

Obedience without emotion is nothing more than discipline or willpower. It is not love. God wants our obedience to always be connected to our love for Him. It is impossible to take passion out of love and still have love. True love will show itself not only in actions, but also in feelings. Affection and passion are indispensable aspects of love for God our Father of our Lord Jesus Christ, and of the love we have for our fellow men.

Dedication through fasting has its place in the body of Christ, just like every other activity in the church. When the leader, Pastor, elder or someone else in leadership asks us to participate in some congregational effort of prayer, worship, counseling, ministering to the poor, evangelical work, or any other way to help, we need to be able to function and perform in the different areas, or we will not be asked to help.

If we are not able to submit through fasting *individually* how can we do it *corporately*? "Accountability" is no longer a popular word, but that's what it takes. A very significant part in a mature Christian life is simple accountability, even in this area.

*Now it came to pass in the fifth year of Jehoiakim the son of
Josiah, king of Judah, in the ninth month, that they proclaimed a fast before the LORD to all the people in Jerusalem,
and to all the people who came from the cities of Judah to
Jerusalem.* (Jeremiah 36:9)

There was no issue about who could fast or who could not, or if it was convenient for all to fast. Everyone should be able to fulfill this, just as they did in Jeremiah 36:9.

Another reason why we should submit through fasting is to humble our souls by self discipline, and the experience we gain leads to maturity. Maturity allows us to exercise our senses, feelings, and minds so that our discernment becomes sensitive. As it says in Psalm 35:13:

I humbled myself with fasting.

There is only one language that our body and soul understands: that is submission through fasting, and when I do it regularly my body and soul will be subject to my will. We need to consider the proper relation between body, soul, and spirit. If I am not in control in all this, then *who* or *what* is? A muscle that is not in use will slowly stop functioning and die.

Spirit, Soul and Body

Let us compare our body with a slave, our soul with a servant, and our spirit with the master. Our *soul* (related to the mind), which is the servant, tells our *body*, which is the slave, to get some good food and some yummy desserts. The slave gets busy and serves the servant, while the master - our *spirit* - is totally denied.

It should be just the opposite. The Master - the *spirit* - should be in charge, and tell the servant - the *soul* - what to do, and the slave - our *body* - will then obey. Paul found that discipline was necessary out of a fear of being disqualified.

I discipline my body like an athlete, training it to do what it should. Otherwise, I fear that after preaching to others I myself might be disqualified. (1 Corinthians 9:27, NLT)

When we are in control of our body, God's holy temple, we will act accordingly and not be disqualified. Remember that there is also a good way to eat and drink because that also is from God, and we should be able to enjoy that as well. God balances these ideas with passage such as Ecclesiastes 2:24:

Nothing is better for a man than that he should eat and drink, and that his soul should enjoy good in his labor. This also, I saw, was from the hand of God.

Warning! Be Aware of the Danger

Craving and appetites are dangerous places to find our selves, when the body - such as our stomach - rules our life. We need to learn the difference between hunger and appetites, to learn how to control our craving, our wants, our desires, and our longing to satisfy our self.

Those who live only to satisfy their own sinful desires will harvest the consequences of decay and death. But those who live to please the Spirit will harvest everlasting life from the Spirit. (Galatians 6:8, NLT)

The food channels on television and all the gourmet cookbooks don't help us in this area, not to mention all the restaurants. Remember that there is nothing wrong with a normal healthy outlook on good healthy food. But some people live to eat, and others eat to live. We are now dealing with *cravings* and *wrong desires*. Follow carefully as we will see how God handles this issue:

So they ate and were well filled, for He gave them their own desire. They were not deprived of their craving; but while their food was still in their mouths, the wrath of God came against them, and slew the stoutest of them, and struck down the choice men of Israel. (Psalm 78:29-31)

The word *stoutest* comes from the ancient Hebrew word *mashman*, which means "fattest." We should read this, *And He slew the fattest of them.* As we look at the word *craving* it means to *demand, an intense, urgent or abnormal desire or longing appetite, itch, lust, passion, or urge.*

Maybe our regular habits have become abnormal by they way they appear. We might like to disregard this passage because it relates to a special situation in the Old Testament. But isn't it true that we can not disregard any place in the Bible? We will find out that the Scripture explains Scripture, from the Old to the New.

These events happened as a warning to us, so that we would not crave evil things as they did. (1 Corinthians 10:6)

Does that mean that food is the same as *evil things*? It is not the food in itself that is evil, it is our attitude towards the food.

When we have an abnormal desire, a desire that rules us, then foods become *evil things*, or whatever else that occupies us.

We are reminded in James 1:14 (NLT) that *Temptation comes from the lure of our own evil desires*, and we can read the whole event in Numbers 11.

Notice the difference. Appetites and cravings relate to the immediate "wants" and "habits" of the mind through our feelings and customs. True hunger, relates to the real need of the body. Do you understand the difference?

We need to learn the difference between hunger and appetite, and learn to control our cravings, our wants, our desires, our longing to satisfy our self. Of course food is necessary for the sustaining of life, but *air*, *water*, and *sleep* are much more urgently needed.

Our body cannot live more that *a few minutes without air*, or a *few days without water and sleep*. But in normal circumstances it can exist quite satisfactory *for several weeks without food*. That is food for thought. A normal healthy and well-nourished body can exist for *several weeks without being injured or incapacitated by lack of food*, that is a well-known fact and has been proven over and over throughout history.

Idolatry is an excessive attachment to something. Is *idolatry* actually relevant to this issue? Yes it is, when we look at what the word means.

And do not become idolaters as were some of them. As it is written, "The people sat down to eat and drink, and rose up to play." (1 Corinthians 10:7)

If our spirit is not in control when it comes to our body and soul in this area of our life, then try to answer this question: When is it in control?

If you reject criticism, you only harm yourself; but if you listen to correction, you grow in understanding. Fear of the LORD teaches a person to be wise; humility precedes honor. (Proverbs 15:32-33, NLT)

A Warning against Living for the Flesh

That Apostle Paul is very determined when he states that we should follow his example, and pay attention to people who walk in the way that should be our pattern:

Brethren, join in following my example, and note those who so walk, as you have us for a pattern. (Philippians 3:17)

Therefore I urge you, imitate me. (1 Corinthians 4:16)

Imitate me, just as I also imitate Christ. (1 Corinthians 11:1)

Following Paul in regard to fasting would be an easy task, because Paul fasted often.

If we are too much set on the flesh or earthly things, to the point that our priorities are out of focus, then we could be in danger. It is dangerous when our godliness becomes a hobby or just something to do on occasion, not affecting our lifestyle.

For I have told you often before, and I say it again with tears in my eyes, that there are many whose conduct shows they are really enemies of the cross of Christ. Their future is eternal destruction. Their god is their appetite, they brag about shameful things, and all they think about is this life here on earth. (Philippians 3:18-19, NLT)

We may not recognize that description, saying that our appetite is our god or that we brag about the way we live, but our attitude and conduct shows if this is true or not. Our response might be, "I am not an enemy of the cross, so this does not apply to me." Remember that the Word of God is sharper than a two-edged sword and is a discerner of our hearts. If the evidence is there, either we admit it or we do not. But we need to listen to the warning because it is very clear. We may react by saying that we did not know that it was so serious. It is good that we react in some way, so please pay attention to what we read in Philippians 3:19:

Their future is eternal destruction.

In contrast, God promises great blessing to those who put Him first, including the area of devotion through fasting.

Whoever offers praise glorifies Me; and to him who orders his conduct aright I will show the salvation of God.
(Psalm 50:23)

May God's mercy and peace be upon all those who live by this principle. They are the new people of God.
(Galatians 6:16, NLT)

When we love and obey our Father and God, nothing matters if we don't do it out of love and devotion to Him. If it does come from love and devotion, then we will conduct our life rightly and live by His principles, showing dedication through fasting regularly because that is His will for us to be holy.

Here again we have to be concerned with what goes on in our mind. Always remember that our mind is the battlefield, not our stomach.

For those who live according to the flesh set their minds on the things of the flesh, but those who live according to the Spirit, the things of the Spirit. For to be carnally minded is death, but to be spiritually minded is life and peace . . . So then, those who are in the flesh cannot please God. For if you live according to the flesh you will die; but if by the Spirit you put to death the deeds of the body, you will live.
(Romans 8:5-6, 8)

So what goes on in our mind is a serious matter, because it can lead to death. Not just any kind of fasting will save us out of the situations we are warned about, but by yielding through fasting we will be more aware of what we must do with our lives. In order to dedicate our self through fasting, we must make some changes in our lifestyle. That in turn will get us started to reflect and continue to become spiritually minded, which will lead to submitted dedication.

Part Five
How We Should Fast

How We Should Fast

Simply, we should fast according to the way Jesus told us:

And when you fast, don't make it obvious, as the hypocrites do, who try to look pale and disheveled so people will admire them for their fasting. I assure you, that is the only reward they will ever get. But when you fast, comb your hair and wash your face. Then no one will suspect you are fasting, except your Father, who knows what you do in secret. And your Father, who knows all secrets, will reward you.
(Matthew 6:16-18, NLT)

When Jesus taught, "Then no one will suspect you are fasting," it means that you should go on with your day as usual, go to work, continue your day according to your daily routine whatever that might be, even if it requires hard labor or sharp concentration. No one should be able to suspect that you are fasting.

My experience is that the first two weeks of fasting do not create any problem. In fact my energy-level is increasing and I am able to accomplish more, and my focus is more intense.

It has been explained to me that during a period of fasting we are not using any energy to digest our food and that means that we have all that extra energy to use, because there is nothing that requires more energy than digesting food. That is the reason we feel sluggish after a big meal.

Because our body is not digesting food it does not generate as much heat. Therefore remember to keep warm during your fast.

Of course, some people close to you will notice that you are not eating. Explaining this to a Christian might be fairly easy, but explaining it to other people may be a challenge, especially if you have been a Christian for a long time and all of a sudden become a Christian who is dedicated through fasting.

Without making a big deal out of it, this may give you an opportunity to share your belief in a loving way. The alternative is to start your fasting on your day off. Jesus taught that we should fast by keeping it a secret, when He said, "what you do in *secret*."

If it is your responsibility to cook food or be engaged in handling food, don't use that as an excuse to take the day off from fasting. Food is not the problem. When you have set your mind to fast, then your thoughts should not be occupied with anything but the Lord and His kingdom. I know that it takes some time and training, and in the learning remember:

And everyone who has this hope in Him purifies himself, just as He is pure. (1 John 3:3)

Family Matters

It is necessary that our immediate family is informed. We are not to keep our regular dedication through fasting a secret from them. We can not keep our fasting a secret from them and it is not our intention to do so, and we especially don't want to keep it a secret from our mates. It is important to establish the right days so it does not create irritation or misunderstanding. Flexibility and consideration should mark our lifestyle even more now.

The Sex Life

Do not deprive one another except with consent for a time, that you may give yourselves to fasting and prayer; and come together again so that Satan does not tempt you because of your lack of self-control. (1 Corinthians 7:5)

It is just as easy to choose time to fast as it is to choose time for any other activity and if we do it on a regular basis we will function in all our activities as usual. We should not need to change anything in our ordinary lifestyle except when it comes to sex. That does not mean that your sex drive stops functioning because you are fasting a few days but that it needs to be disciplined.

I say then: Walk in the Spirit, and you shall not fulfill the lust of the flesh. (Galatians 5:16)

There is nothing dramatic or over-religious about dedication through fasting, so let us act like mature believers and take control over our body, or something else will control us. Let us be doers of the Word in a Biblical manner like the Apostle Paul wrote in 1 Corinthians 9:27. I just quoted it, but it needs repeating:

I discipline my body like an athlete, training it to do what it should. Otherwise, I fear that after preaching to others I myself might be disqualified. (1 Corinthians 9:27, NLT)

I have found this next piece of advice very important. *You must choose a time to start and a time to stop.* Be specific, exactly on the hour, because that will save you a lot of battles - just stick to your decision. I have experienced that when I set a definite time my body automatically accepts and adjusts in a natural way and then the hunger pains are radically reduced, because my body now expects my spirit to be in control. This is because we were made to have the spirit in control, and this brings harmony and peace in His Temple, which is my body.

Never let your feelings, your body, your five senses, or your soul set the time when you should start or stop a time of fasting. Always let your spirit set the time period.

The main reason for dedication through fasting is to draw near to our Father and God, and to be equipped and fitted to live in accord with the Word of God in a humble and obedient way.

Is it Possible to Feel Good through Fasting?

Definitely and undoubtedly, the answer is "Yes." I would not say so if I did not know this by experience. It might take a while, but once this good feeling is there it never leaves. Fasting does not take away any of our ability to be happy or to mourn. We are, of course, able to act anyway that we usually do. Jesus said, "That you do not appear to men to be fasting." That is what matters.

Thus says the LORD of hosts: "The fast of the fourth month, the fast of the fifth, the fast of the seventh, and the fast of the tenth, shall be joy and gladness and cheerful feasts for the house of Judah. Therefore love truth and peace."
(Zechariah 8:19)

We cannot be reminded too often that submission through fasting is not what we are aiming at. It is just the *way* to a complete lifestyle, because that kind of lifestyle does not harm us in any way, but the opposite is true. In spite of the way many people think submission through fasting is a godly way of living that brings dedication and devotion to our lives. It is not a great sacrifice but a normal reasonable service.

When NOT to Fast

If you have any kind of sickness or are taking some medication; if you are pregnant or breastfeeding, then I recommend that you first talk to a doctor before fasting. Preferably, talk to a doctor that knows about fasting.

However, do not let a regular cold or flu or congestion stop you from fasting. There are some studies that show that fasting will enhance the recovery of certain illnesses and how important it is for the body to have a time of detoxification. But as I stated earlier the only reason to fast should be when God in His Word directs us to fast, but not primarily for the health benefits. However, many severe illnesses have been cured through God's intervention by prayer and fasting, through proper guidance from people that are experienced in that particular area.

How Often Should We Fast?

Does the Bible tell us in a direct number of days and how often we should fast?

At the time of Jesus, the Scriptures tell us that some religious people fasted two days a week (Luke 18:12).

This question is directly related to *why* I fast, and if I do it according to the Word of God. If we remember that the main reason for dedication through fasting is not to do it for itself, but we do it in order to draw near to Him, to be equipped and fitted according to His direction. Could anyone of us set a limit to that desire in us? I have experienced that the more I receive from Him the more I need Him. When does too much dedication through fasting stand in the way of spiritual achievement and maturity, or keep us from being equipped and fitted?

Remember it is a way, not a goal. Use the way to victory.

For every child of God defeats this evil world by trusting Christ to give the victory. (1 John 5:4, NLT)

When we persist in these disciplines as part of our lifestyle, it will make us even more firmly established. If we really seek understanding we will receive this wise counsel.

The advice of the wise (those mature in Christ) *is like a life-giving fountain; those who accept it avoid the snares of death.* (Proverbs 13:14, NLT)

We are excellent, good servants when we receive this wisdom and let it flow from our life like a life-giving fountain.

When dedication through fasting and prayer becomes a part of our life as a constant repeated routine it is then more than a lifestyle, it even becomes an asset. I can truly testify to the truth of that. When the Lord promises a reward, it certainly touches all areas of our life.

Good Advice

I recommend that if you never have fasted before, then do not overdo it. Start out with only one day a week and gradually go on to two or three days. On some occasions do three days up to a week, depending on your personal need or as the Church asks you to. When you discover what a wonderful way God has released by dedication through fasting, you will go on to some longer periods such as 10 to 40 days twice a year.

Again I like to quote Martin Luther: "One should not fast in order to do a good deed, but only, and I mean only, in order to be equipped and fit to live in accordance with the Word of God."

To be prepared and fitted to live in accordance with the Word of God is a goal that we all have, but perhaps dedication through fasting and prayer has not been on our agenda.

This will end the last portion of who, why, and how we should fast, and now we will enter the practical recommendations that are based on my experience and study since 1986 on a continual, weekly basis.

Practical Advice on Fasting Regularly

If you never fasted before, I have a few recommendations for you. In your preparation to get started, choose a day to start your fast such as after supper at six in the evening. As an example, if you have chosen to fast for forty hours, that means you will break your fast the second day at 10:00 in the morning. Later on I will explain how to break a fast and to start eating again.

In any case, it is very important to *drink water*! Especially if you never fasted before, start out with drinking a lot of water. It is good to drink at least two quarts a day. It's a good thing to do even when you are not fasting, because it will help when you start your fast. If you fast for three days or more I will recommend three to five quarts a day. Don't take this as a rule, just as a good recommendation. Remember - the water should be of good quality, not ice-cold, and keep track of how much you are drinking. In fact warm water has a tendency to make your hunger disappear. I have experienced that if I use some lemon juice to make the water taste better, the hunger will be kept alive, so there is no benefit in that. Pure water is best. As I mentioned before, remember to consult your doctor (it is always better if he understands fasting) if you have some form of sickness or if you take medication.

When you fast for three days or longer it is good to take a mild laxative, preferably a natural laxative, such as Magnesium Citrate Oral Solution or 1½ ounces of Glauber's salt in 1¼ pints of warm water the day before, to cleanse out your body. That will help your system because there is a cleansing process going on, and it will benefit your colon and the bowel, which is a twisted tube some 25 feet long, and it takes an average of about 24 hours to discharge its contents. Laxatives are not recommended once the fast is underway.

Withdrawal

Perhaps you drink too much coffee, tea, cola, or other drinks that contain caffeine or alcohol. Maybe you eat a lot of sweets, candy, chocolates, ice cream, or deserts. These things can cause you to experience withdrawal when you fast - problems like headaches, dizziness, an upset stomach, or feeling generally uncomfortable. This is a cleansing of all the poisons that your body has taken in. Are you aware that chocolates contain small amounts of cannabinoids from cannabis? These chemicals are the active ingredients in marijuana.

An average adult may eat as much as one and a half pounds of deadly poisons a year. Because of this, the body reacts and does not want you to change your habits and take command over your body. When these feelings come, your desire to fast may fade away and all kinds of rebellion and desires are awakened. This is why it is so important that your mind be renewed, and that your strength comes from within, that you are in Christ and in Him you can do all things who strengthens you. This is why it is important to build a solid foundation through preparation and submission.

Stand firm in your conviction. Persevere in the battle! Whatever you do, continue for the duration of the time you set out to fast. You are not going to die. If you allow the body to win the first battle, it will be so much harder to overcome the next time. Remember that it will become better as you continue, and the bad feelings will pass away. We are all so different, and we live different lifestyles, so you may not experience any problems at all. Remember that your goal is worthwhile: to become holy and acceptable before Him in love. Be aware that the enemy will use all different kind of avenues to discourage you, even if it is just to make you procrastinate your debut to dedicate yourself through fasting on a regular basis. Do not seek support for your decision from anyone, not even from clergy - I am sorry to say - because of the ignorance that flourishes in this area of dedication. Follow my advice and let the Holy Spirit lead you all the way. Renew your mind and become more like Him.

Yes, and all who desire to live godly in Christ Jesus will suffer persecution. (2 Timothy 3:12)

Many are the afflictions of the righteous, but the LORD delivers him out of them all. (Psalm 34:19)

The deliverance is there if I choose to accept it.

Even after years of fasting regularly, I am persuaded that I will constantly battle with the temptation to break my habit, to call it off and live an ordinary dual life like I lived before. It is a constant battle that will remain as long as I remain in this body.

Usually you will notice hunger pains at the normal time for your meal. You can ease the hunger by drinking water. Do not let yourself be possessed with the thought of food. Talk to your body and let the body know that you are obeying your Father and His Word. Glorify Him through meditation and prayer.

Mark out a straight path for your feet.

It is amazing how wonderful it will work out when you have the right preparation. When you rely on His guidance and your yielding, and you give yourself in love to Him in a reasonable service. There is nothing difficult or impossible in following Jesus, the Word - believe me I know. Even if you feel you should have done this long ago, you should not feel any guilt or condemnation; instead count yourself as privileged, and know that you are now being trained in the right way according to the Master Jesus Christ.

Now you have been given all that you need to be obedient in following the Holy Spirit's leading to accomplish what He teaches in the Word. Receive comfort in the following words:

No discipline is enjoyable while it is happening - it is painful! But afterward there will be a quiet harvest of right living for those who are trained in this way. So take a new grip with your tired hands and stand firm on your shaky legs. Mark out a straight path for your feet. Then those who follow you, though they are weak and lame, will not stumble and fall but will become strong. (Hebrews 12:11-13, NLT)

How Your Body May React

Normally, in a longer fast there are three stages that we go through. Here again it varies from person to person and how much we pay attention. If you focus on how your body will react you will notice these three stages, even when they tend to overlap and though the duration of each stage may vary.

The first phase occurs between three and six days, and is characterized by a craving for food (you might like to call it hunger). As you make holiness through fasting more and more a part of your life, the easier this phase will become. You might find yourself indulging in dreams about pleasurable taste sensations but these will pass, and as you choose not to think in that direction, the craving will fade.

The second stage happens between the seventh and eleventh day. This is a phase that I have never experienced to be very strong. It is marked by a feeling of weakness and faintness, and has a direct relation to your everyday eating habits. My personal experience is that my energy level increases up through two weeks of fasting. But as I pointed out earlier, everyone is different. Some people might find it necessary to rest a good deal until this phase has passed. The gradual disappearance of this sense of weakness is a signal that the body has eliminated its grosser wastes and poisons.

Remember that a normally healthy and well-nourished body is not injured or incapacitated by lack of food. The body carries on and draws from surplus fat, and at the same time, the body acts like an internal incinerator, burning and melting up the waste and decaying tissues in the body. The body does not stop functioning because we stop eating. In fact it goes on working, and it keeps doing a lot of good. So continue to go to the bathroom, empty your stomach, even when you are not taking in any nourishment.

The third stage is of course the easiest one, because now you will be walking on clouds, or the difficulties you have experienced will decrease and your concerns about food are gone. You will really have the feeling that you can go on fasting indefinitely. The only focus now is to adhere to your commitment regarding when you will break the fast and that might take some effort because you feel so good and your body is at ease, and in tune with your spirit. Your body becomes yielded and comfortable that you have made a decision to act according to the Word.

I strongly recommend not to proceed any longer than 40 days. This third phase might end as early as the 27th day, but usually after 40 days. If the hunger pangs become severe, that is the sign that the process of elimination has been completed and that the body now is beginning to draw on the sound living tissue. Again, usually this happens after 40 days.

This is the "starvation bell" announcing that the body now must have food. It might be the first time you experience some real hunger pains, not just a craving or a desire for some gourmet food for pleasure. This is the "complete fast" and in accordance with what is known as a true fasting process, all the reserves of the body are expended and starvation is setting in.

To be assured that when the Bible refers to exact numbers like the 40-day fasting period, we can compare it with the 8-day period from when a baby is born to when they circumcise the baby, according to Scripture. It is proven that the levels of vitamin K and prothrombin are at their highest level on the 8th day, and these help cause the blood to clot so a cut can mend and heal, closing the wound from receiving infection. Our body is wonderfully made. We can trust our Maker's direction, and know that if He has the wisdom to prescribe 8 days until circumcision, He knows our bodies can handle up to 40 days of fasting.

Hygiene During the Time of Fasting

As I mentioned before, the body goes through a cleansing process. In some cases it will create odors, so it might be good to take an extra shower now and then. Also, do not forget your mouth, because fasting can give you bad breath. Because we keep contact with people during a fast, I recommend using some breath mints that do not contain sugar.

Jesus made these principles clear when He said in the Sermon on the Mount:

> *But when you fast, comb your hair and wash your face.*
> (Matthew 6:17, NLT)

Attitude, Spirituality, and Sleep

It has been my experience that when I fast, I find it easier to control my attitude, regardless in what situation I find myself. It seems that patience and self-control are enhanced among many other positive experiences, and I sense a wonderful over-all well-being from within.

When I am on a longer fast (ten days or more) I do not need as much sleep and when I do sleep, it is always a very light sleep. I find that I have much more time to draw near to Him through meditation on His Word and by memorizing His promises.

Does fasting enhance spirituality? Yes, but that has a direct relationship to how much I meditate, pray, praise, read, and study the Bible during the time of the fast. Fasting itself may not enhance spirituality, but those actions come easier when I am dedicated through fasting.

A Warning for Former Drug Addicts

Former drug users have told me that on a longer fast they some-times experience flashbacks. This is because during a fast, we often become more sensitive to the whole spirit realm, includ-ing the evil spirit realm. So if there is some area that we not have surrendered to God, it could lead to an unexpected spiri-tual encounter. This is true only if the evil forces already have some hold or some avenues in a person's life. I am not talking about common sins; they will not necessarily leave a person sensitive or open for satanic impressions when they are in-volved in longer fasts.

When such a flashback happens, it is often the first step to dealing with the problem in a constructive way, and by that I mean to be completely delivered and set free. We have no rea-son to be crippled by fear, by the fear that we will become more vulnerable when we fast. We have nothing to fear as we remember when Jesus fasted for 40 days and nights and en-countered the Devil, and each time He replied: "IT IS WRITTEN."

Of course we should always be clothed with the full armor of God like as Paul wrote about in Ephesians:

Therefore take up the whole armor of God, that you may be able to withstand in the evil day, and having done all, to stand. (Ephesians 6:13)

If we humbly and obediently follow Gods direction in fasting, will He reward us with an encounter with the devil? Definitely not. His rewards always benefit His children in a wonderful and loving way.

Fasting as Spiritual Exercise

Physical exercise has some value, but spiritual exercise is much more important, for it promises a reward in both this life and the next. This is true, and everyone should accept it . . . Teach these things and insist that everyone learn them.
(1 Timothy 4:8, 11, NLT)

Dedication through fasting is something that is good, positive and reassuring both for your self-image and for your faith. Remember that dedication through fasting and prayer in itself is not what we aim for, but it certainly is God's road to travel.

How to Break Your Fast and Start Eating Again

The term "breakfast" comes from the Biblical phrase "breaking the fast." In John 21:12, according to *The Interlinear Greek-English New Testament*, "Jesus said to them, 'Come break fast.'"

If we have fasted for one or two days, it is usually no problem to break the fast and start eating again. Regardless of how many days you fast, it will always seems like you never will get enough food the first day. It takes a lot of restraint and you should consider the first day after your fast as if it belonged to your fast, so the breaking of a fast is actually a part of the fasting period. During this time, restrain your eating to your regular mealtimes. Do not overindulge. Learn to restrain your appetite, especially on the first day. The second day your body is back to normal. However, you can not count the breaking-day as a fasting day. When you break after three days or more of fasting it is important that you continue to drink a lot of water. Now that your fast is over, it is the time to drink fruit juices and vegetable drinks.

When you break a longer fast, start out with some prunes soaked in water so they are moist and soft. Tomatoes with the skin removed by boiling them in water are also good. Be careful with your appetite. Remember the fast is not over yet, and it is now that self-discipline is so valuable to apply.

Now you may start with some lean soup. Eat small portions, eat fruit and continue to drink a lot of water. After a few times you will get the hang of it and create your own way to break a longer fast. When you have fasted for ten days or more, you might find it difficult to break the fast because you feel so good and the hunger pains are no longer present, and food is no longer on your mind. Often in a longer fast the desire for food seems totally gone.

These experiences can be different from person to person. It might occur after 8 days or it might happen after 15 days, differing from person to person. I mention it so that you will be aware, because you have chosen a time to stop your fast and you are confident that you are in control and your body knows it because you are determined. As you go on, follow these instructions about how to break a fast, act upon your decision, regardless of your feelings. Remember, never let your body, soul, or mind determine when you should start or stop a time of fasting. That is guidance that you need from the spirit.

After a long fast, you may desire some solid food. It is very important to take it slowly, to be careful and to wait a couple of days before moving on to solid food. Don't eat anything that is tough for the stomach to digest. Eat at your regular mealtimes. Fresh vegetables and fruits are good choices. Your heart is now filled with thanksgiving for all God did in your life during this longer fast. When you start to eat again, you might be all consumed with what you eat the first time and your sense of awareness is now at its peak. Learn to automatically eat slowly and to masticate (chew) well. Everything tastes so good and you might discover some new taste sensations. Be sure to rejoice and enjoy your eating. Give thanks to God and praise Him for the food.

After a fast it is the ideal time to stop some bad eating habits, maybe to stop drinking coffee, and definitely to stop putting a lot of poison in your body. Use your awakened awareness to benefit your spirit, body, and soul, because the Holy Spirit likes to help your total being. The tendency to be more careful about your eating habits and your overall feeling for order and cleanliness is something that many people experience. The saying, "Cleanliness is next to godliness" must have originated from a person who fasted. To get read of some bad habits is good, but it is much more rewarding to embrace good and godly habits.

According to the Apostle Paul in 2 Corinthians, he lived his life like this:

In weariness and toil, in sleeplessness often, in hunger and thirst, in fastings often, in cold and nakedness.
(2 Corinthians 11:27-28)

Regardless of what situations and circumstances Paul and his companions found themselves in, they fasted often. It was their lifestyle. That means that once we have received the light over an area that requires a lifestyle change such as dedication through fasting we should not let anything block our way as we carry out our conviction. We should not let any circumstance become an excuse. To procrastinate now is to harden our heart. A faith that does not produce real change in our conduct is a dead faith. That is why renewing our mind will cause change to take place and our lifestyle will become more Christ-like.

Allowing Godly Habits to Reshape our Lifestyle

It is more important to take on new godly habits than it is to work on the old ones. When we renew our mind, there will not be any room for old habits. Yes, we need to allow ourselves to take advantage of what devotion through fasting will accomplish in us. Then our Father will reward us as Jesus taught. Let this teaching about regular dedication through fasting, founded on the Word of God, become rooted and grounded in you, and use the Word to build your faith, and let the fruit become the evidence in your lives as Paul says in Galatians:

> *Don't be misled. Remember that you can't ignore God and get away with it. You will always reap what you sow! Those who live only to satisfy their own sinful desires will harvest the consequences of decay and death. But those who live to please the Spirit will harvest everlasting life from the Spirit. So don't get tired of doing what is good. Don't get discouraged and give up, for we will reap a harvest of blessing at the appropriate time.* (Galatians 6:7-9, NLT)

The Length of Time We Should be Able to Fast

> *Go, gather all the Jews who are present in Shushan, and fast for me; neither eat nor drink for three days, night or day. My maids and I will fast likewise. And so I will go to the king, which is against the law; and if I perish, I perish!*
> (Esther 4:16)

We should be able to fast according to the pattern the Spirit establishes in our life. As we fast when He moves us, this will sometimes mean a longer or more intense fast. This passage in Esther 4 shows an especially intense fast, where they did "neither eat nor drink" - that means no food or liquid - for three days. Notice that this fast was specifically practiced to accomplish something and to make the difference in a desperate situation. But what a victorious result! I found it easier to fast without water.

The Scriptures also describes some other fasts that were for more than just a day.

Then they took their bones and buried them under the
tamarisk tree at Jabesh, and fasted seven days.
(1 Samuel 31:13)

So it was, when I heard these words, that I sat down and
wept, and mourned for many days; I was fasting and praying
before the God of heaven. (Nehemiah 1:4)

The Bible shows that no one fasted for more than 40 days and nights. Our life, our spiritual walk as a Christian, must be rooted and directed through our spiritual wealth. As Paul emphasized in the book of Romans, behavior does not determine blessing, instead blessing should determine behavior.

And you He made alive, who were dead in trespasses and
sins, in which you once walked according to the course of
this world, according to the prince of the power of the air,
the spirit who now works in the sons of disobedience, among
whom also we all once conducted ourselves in the lusts of
our flesh, fulfilling the desires of the flesh and of the mind,
and were by nature children of wrath, just as the others.
(Ephesians 2:1-3)

We are not just as the others any longer, we are different, and we are a new creation. We are not to fulfill the regular desires of the flesh and the mind any longer. Our time is spent in a much different manner than the people of the world, the people who do not have Christ as their Lord. We are different because we live under grace, not under wrath. We are called to be free, to live powerfully, victoriously and in charge of our body, which is the temple of our God. Our attitude and our actions - our lifestyle if you will - reveals our faith. A genuine faith will produce real changes in our conduct and character.

The absence of change is a symptom of a dead faith. We might say that a faith that produces no change is not a saving faith. When was the last time your faith made a permanent change in your lifestyle? When did it last make a change not only in the way that you think, but actually made you *act* differently?

Consecration through Fasting

We will take a look at three Bible passages that speak very clearly about consecration. In the Old Testament, the word "consecration" comes from the Hebrew word *gadash* meaning, "to make, pronounce, or observe as clean (ceremonially or morally), to dedicate, hallow, holy, purify, to sanctify one's self."

"Now, therefore," says the LORD, "Turn to Me with all your heart, with fasting, with weeping, and with mourning."
(Joel 2:12)

Then Moses said, "Consecrate yourselves today to the LORD, that He may bestow on you a blessing this day."
(Exodus 32:29)

Consecrate yourselves therefore, and be holy, for I am the LORD your God. (Leviticus 20:7)

What this means is obvious. To dedicate or to set one's self apart means "renewal." Every so often we come to the conclusion that we need to do something again, like renewing our vows to the Lord or to do something to get refreshed in our dedication. That is why the phrase *consecration* through *fasting* is used in order to sustain our effort and make a difference. To consecrate a fast to the Lord is a mature act of sanctification, dedication, purification, and humble obedience.

Conclusion: Dedication through Fasting Matters

Obedience is not negotiable. Dedication through fasting is an act of obedience. In the beginning we asked a simple question: Does dedication through fasting and prayer matter? The answer is simple. Fasting matters because the Bible matters.

Here are four basic practices on our way to maturity in Christ.

　　1. I am born again and I experience and practice freedom in Christ through faith. I am immersed, baptized in

water and I have received the baptism in the Holy Spirit, and I am daily including unknown tongues in times of fellowship with my Father.

2. My dedication is to constantly practice a lifestyle that consists of yielding, awareness, and submission to be equipped and fitted by the Holy Spirit's leading so that I can become more useful for His body, the Church. One of the consequences is that I am studying and thinking on the Word of God on a regular basis, by the hour.

3. By the Word and my heart's conviction, in a thankful humble obedience I want to offer my body as a living sacrifice, for a reasonable service. I do this through devoted fasting at least once a week on a regular basis.

4. I am being filled with the Holy Spirit and renewing my mind, offering the sacrifice of praise and thanksgiving through devoted submission every day.

For every child of God defeats this evil world by trusting Christ to give the victory. And the ones who win this battle against the world are the ones who believe that Jesus is the Son of God. (1 John 5:4-5, NLT)

He, the Son of God our Redeemer, Teacher and Master fasted and taught us to fast.

A disciple is not above his teacher, but everyone who is perfectly trained will be like his teacher.
(Luke 6:40)

But whoever keeps His word, truly the love of God is perfected in him. By this we know that we are in Him.
(1 John 2:5)

He who says he abides in Him ought himself also to walk just as He walked.

What a marvelous and wonderful way the Holy Spirit opens up our spiritual eyes to see the truth about dedication through fasting! If we now choose the freedom we are called to walk in, we can truly and willingly surrender to His leadership as

Jesus said in John 14:23:

All those who love me will do what I say.

Let us repeat the prayer we started with, taken from Psalm 119:12 and 119:15-17 (NLT).

- *Blessed are you, O LORD; teach me your principles* (about dedication through fasting)
- *I will study your commandments and reflect on your ways, I will delight in your principles and not forget your Word* (about dedication through fasting)
- *Be good to your servant, that I may live and obey your Word, open my eyes to see the wonderful truths in your law* (about dedication through fasting)

"Father, God of our Lord Jesus Christ I ask You to continue to reveal, strengthen, and confirm Your will in my life through the Holy Spirit's leading. I ask that You may give to me the Spirit of wisdom and revelation in the knowledge of Him. I also pray that You will perfect my reasonable service so that the eyes of my understanding will be enlightened in the area of dedication through fasting and prayer so I will become in tune with the Word You planted in my heart and my renewed mind, according to the exceeding greatness of Your mighty power that works in me. Being perfectly trained, I will be more and more like my teacher, Jesus Christ. Thank You, Father of our Lord Jesus Christ, in His name I pray, amen and amen."

Dedication - Offer a Promise – Make a Commitment to the Life Giving Light of Truth About Fasting and Become More like Christ

Through devoted dedication and submitted yielding to God's clear message about practical and spiritual holiness through reasonable service by regular prayer and fasting,

I will fulfill my vows to you, O God, and offer a sacrifice of thanks for your help. For you have rescued me from death; you have kept my feet from slipping. So now I can walk in your presence, O God, in your life-giving light.
(Psalm 56:12-13, NLT)

It is important to make a choice and to start acting on your knowledge and conviction. I may not know you by name, but I will pray for those who read this book and are led to make a commitment to dedicated and regular prayer and fasting.

Your commitment should be to follow the Word of God in this area of dedication through prayer and fasting regularly, and to make it your lifestyle. Make up your mind when you want to start - choose one day a week, or however the Lord may lead you - being sensitive to the Spirit's leading is what matters. The main object is to act, and to act now. Genuine faith means being a doer of the Word. Procrastination is a road to defeat.

When you submit to a commitment like this, it is very good to be accountable to a person, preferably someone that lives according to these principles themselves. But it is even more important to remember that God, our heavenly Father is involved in your promise. He is the One you commit to, because of your love for Him. It is His Word - Jesus Christ - that you must follow and obey. Let the Holy Spirit guide your heart.

My prayer is that this book about dedication to regular prayer and fasting has enlightened you to the point that God's Word now is making you act, and that He would grant you according to the riches of His glory to be strengthened with might through His Spirit in your inner man and that Christ may continue to dwell in your heart through faith. May the God of our Lord Jesus Christ sanctify and complete the good work He began in you and is enhancing through your commitment to humbly obey. Amen and amen.

But whoever keeps His word, truly the love of God is perfected in him. By this we know that we are in Him. He who says he abides in Him ought himself also to walk just as He walked. (1 John 2:5-6, NLT)

Jesus replied, "All those who love me will do what I say. My Father will love them, and we will come to them and live with them." (John 14:23)

Questions and Answers About Fasting and Prayer

QUESTIONS

1. Romans 12:1 tells Christians to *present your bodies a living sacrifice, holy, acceptable to God, which is your reasonable service*. In what way does that Scripture apply to fasting?

2. How do we carry out according to Scripture "reasonable service" through dedication to fasting and prayer?

3. What is the most essential part of our preparation to become dedicated through prayer and fasting as a regular part of our lifestyle?

4. What can straighten us out, and teach us to do what is right in every area, including submission to prayer and fasting on a regular basis?

5. Is having a good motivation the same as renewing our mind?

6. Does obedience play an essential role in our endeavor to devotion by prayer and fasting on a regular basis?

7. What does the word *fasting* mean?

8. Who should be dedicated through prayer and fasting on a regular basis?

9. Why should we be dedicated through prayer and fasting on a regular basis?

10. What is practical spirituality?

11. Is faith an activity in our *body*, in our *soul*, or in our *spirit*?

12. When will God direct our path, or our life?

13. In Daniel 10:2 and 3 we read that Daniel was mourning for three weeks. Was that a regular fast?

14. Does God teach us by hunger? What kind of food, should we take in to have real life?

15. What three things should we be warned against when we plan to be obedient to the Word of God, and to submit to prayer and fasting?

16. What does the Bible say to those who reject criticism?

17. If we know that we are going to do hard labor or work that requires concentration, is that a reason to discontinue or not go ahead and plan a fasting-period?

18. Should we keep our fasting a secret?

19. How should I know when to start or stop a time of fasting?

20. Can we be "up" and happy during a time of fasting?

21. Does the Scripture set any limit to how many days we should fast a week?

22. What should determine how often we fast?

23. Is dedication through fasting and prayer on a regular basis a sign of maturity?

24. When is it advisable to contact a doctor before fasting?

25. Is it advisable to take laxatives during fast?

26. Does the Scripture recommend fasting as a way to conquer a person's evil thoughts and desires?

27. Is dedication through fasting and prayer a spiritual exercise?

28. How soon after a longer fast can I eat solid food?

29. Does it take any special food to break a fast lasting one or two days?

30. Why does regular dedication through fasting and prayer matter?

31. Does Jesus actually say that we should fast?

32. Where does temptation come from, including the temptation to neglect fasting and prayer on a regular basis?

33. Is it possible to undo or pay for our sin through fasting?

34. In what areas of my individual Christian life does dedication through fasting support me?

35. What are the consequences if I am not able to keep on fasting on a regular basis, as the Word teaches, and end up feeling guilty?

ANSWERS

1. **Answer:** Reasonable service describes fasting by the definition of what *reasonable service* is. We remember that *reasonable* means:

1. To be within reason	6. Restrained
2. Not asking too much	7. Unextreme
3. Logical	8. Controlled
4. Sensible	9. Moderate
5. Sound	

Each of these applies to fasting both in what it is and what it does.

2. **Answer:** Fasting is connected to reasonable service because it happens in ministry unto the Lord, and in ministry unto men. Acts 13:2-3 reminds us of this:

As they ministered to the Lord and fasted, the Holy Spirit said, "Now separate to Me Barnabas and Saul for the work to which I have called them." Then, having fasted and prayed, and laid hands on them, they sent them away.

We see from this that fasting was connected with their ministry to the Lord, and also connected with ministry to others in their calling.

3. **Answer:** The most important part of preparation is to renew our mind by changing the way we think about eating, appetite, food and hunger, according to the principle of Romans 12:1-2.

4. **Answer:** All Scripture teaches us and sraightens us out.

All Scripture is inspired by God and is useful to teach us what is true and to make us realize what is wrong in our lives. It straightens us out and teaches us to do what is right.
(2 Timothy 3:16, NLT)

Can we apply this to fasting? Why not?

5. **Answer:** Absolutely not; good motivation is not the same thing as renewing our mind.

6. **Answer:** Of course obedience is important. If I am obedient to the Word of God I will devote myself in this area. If I don't, does this mean that I am disobedient? The answer is "yes."

7. **Answer:** "Fasting" means to abstain from solid or liquid food, for a set period of time, usually 24 hours or more. On some occasions fasting means even going without water.

8. **Answer:** Anyone who is a child of God should be concerned with regular fasting and prayer.

9. **Answer:** There are three reasons to be dedicated to fasting and prayer.

- Because it belongs to our service and ministry to our God and Father and to the Body of Christ, the Church
- To be equipped and fitted to live according to the Word of God
- To be obedient, according to His direction

10. **Answer:** Practical spirituality is to be transformed by the renewing of our mind, by changing the way we think. *Transformed* means a conversion or a major change, and *convert* implies a change fitting something for a new or different use or function. As well, when the Holy Spirit controls our life, He will produce the fruits of the Spirit, of which there are nine, and there is nothing more practical than that.

11. **Answer:** Faith is an activity that affects all three - body, soul, and spirit.

12. **Answer:** There are three aspects to receiving this direction from God, each based on Proverbs 3:5.

Trust in the LORD with all your heart, and lean not on your own understanding; in all your ways acknowledge Him, and He shall direct your paths.

- God will direct our path when we trust in the Lord with all our heart

- God will direct our path when we do not depend on our own understanding

- God will direct our path when we acknowledge Him in all our ways, including prayer and fasting

13. **Answer:** The Bible does not state that Daniel was really fasting. Look carefully at the passage.

In those days I, Daniel, was mourning three full weeks. I ate no pleasant food, no meat or wine came into my mouth, nor did I anoint myself at all, till three whole weeks were fulfilled. (Daniel 10:2-3)

14. **Answer:** Yes, God does teach us by hunger, based on Deuteronomy 8:3. This same passage shows us that the real food for real life is to feed on every Word of the Lord.

15. **Answer:** We are warned against these three things.

- Craving and appetites

- Any kind of sickness, medication, or pregnancy, or breast-feeding

- Living for the flesh

16. **Answer:** The Bible says that when we reject criticism, we only harm our self. Hear what the Bible says:

If you reject criticism, you only harm yourself; but if you listen to correction, you grow in understanding.
(Proverbs 15:32, NLT)

17. **Answer:** No. We should go ahead and fast, and carry on our regularly planned duties, if the fast is not longer than ten days. But this can vary from person to person.

18. **Answer:** Yes, we should keep our fasting secret, according to what Jesus said in Matthew 6:18:

Then no one will suspect you are fasting, except your Father, who knows what you do in secret. And your Father, who knows all secrets, will reward you.

19. **Answer:** We learn how long to fast by learning to listen to our humble and devoted spirit and to the Holy Spirit. We can not rely on direction from our feelings, our body, our senses, or our soul. None of them should direct us when to start or stop a time of fasting, only the spirit.

20. **Answer:** Yes. The Bible says that fasting can become a cheerful feast.

Thus says the LORD of hosts: "The fast of the fourth month, the fast of the fifth, the fast of the seventh, and the fast of the tenth, shall be joy and gladness and cheerful feasts for the house of Judah. Therefore love truth and peace."
(Zechariah 8:19)

Fasting does not take away any of our ability for joy.

21. **Answer:** No, there is no limit to how often we should fast.

22. **Answer:** How often we fast should reflect our willingness to get anything out of the way that blocks our spiritual achievement and maturity.

23. **Answer:** Yes, fasting is one sign of maturity, but not the only one.

24. **Answer:** You should contact a doctor before fasting when you have an illness, are taking medication, are pregnant, or if you are breastfeeding.

25. **Answer:** Laxatives are not advised during a fast, only as a preparation for a longer fast, and then use a natural mild ones such as Magnesium Citrate Oral Solution or Glauber's salt.

26. **Answer:** No, fasting in itself does not battle these things - just the opposite. Read what the Word of God says to us in Colossians 2:20-23:

These rules may seem wise because they require strong devotion, humility, and severe bodily discipline. But they have no effect when it comes to conquering a person's evil thoughts and desires. (Colossians 2:20-23, NLT)

27. **Answer:** Yes, fasting and prayer are spiritual exercises.

28. **Answer:** You should wait for two days after a longer fast before eating normal solid foods.

29. **Answer:** No, a shorter fast doesn't require special foods when breaking the fast. But in the beginning of your lifestyle, be careful and do break your fast slowly. But after you have regularly have practiced fasting, you will find that there is no special procedure for breaking a fast of a shorter period.

30. **Answer:** Fasting matters because the Bible matters.

31. **Answer:** Yes, Jesus expected that we would fast, according to Matthew 9:15 (*and then they will fast*) and Matthew 6:16 (*when you fast*).

32. **Answer:** According to James 1:14, temptation comes from *the lure of our own evil desires*.

33. **Answer:** No, fasting can't atone for our sin. Only the work of Jesus can pay for our sin and undo the guilt of sin.

34. **Answer:** Dedication through fasting supports me in Bible study, meditation, praise and worship, prayer, being led by the Holy Spirit, and simply living as the Word of God says I should live. It supports me in all these areas.

35. **Answer:** Depending on your attitude, guilt can be a healthy sense of awareness when you choose to deal with it. When you don't, it can cause your conscience to bother you with symptoms like excuses, cover-ups, disobedience, and lies, which all make you vulnerable. But don't give up, this is not asking too much. It is to be within reason. Through Christ we can do all things.

DEDICATION THROUGH BASIC LESSONS IN PERSONAL PRAYER

Lessons in Prayer - Part One
"OUR FATHER"

Since our goal and purpose is to draw near to our God and Father, into rich fellowship with Him, we need to understand how important prayer is and how God our Father wants us to perform in that area of our life as His children. If we fail to seek God in prayer according to His way and direction, then we deny His purpose for prayer.

What is prayer? Prayer is communicating with our God and Father and communication is a two-way matter, a response of giving and receiving. Our greatest need is to be in constant communication and fellowship with God, to abide in Him, to glorify and praise Him and His Son Jesus Christ. His desire for us is to fulfill our greatest need. That is why the Holy Spirit is so eager to help and guide us. We are going to pursue the area of prayer that Jesus taught the disciples when they asked Him how to pray in Matthew 6:9-13.

INTIMACY REQUIRES DEVELOPMENT

To develop or to achieve fellowship and intimacy with God our Father, we must begin from deep down in our heart. This means spending more time with Him in His presence to discover this ever-increasing delight. We will enjoy and develop that kind of intimacy because we love Him. In His love for us we will receive directions on how to respond and spend time in His presence by the Holy Spirit who guides us. To abide in the anointing we have received through Him means that we will carry out a lifestyle that is focused on making this intimate time come true. To put it plainly, simply start to set time aside to be with Him on a daily schedule. We have order in some areas of our life because we have made a habit of doing things in an orderly way. So now we pursue the same thing in the area of personal prayer.

Colossians 4:2 communicates the need for setting time aside for prayer when it tells us to:

> *Continue earnestly in prayer, being vigilant in it with thanksgiving.*

The word *vigilant* means "being on the alert, watchful and awake." It speaks of *action* as well as *attention*.

Ephesians 6:18 also communicates this idea:

> *Praying always with all prayer and supplication in the Spirit, being watchful to this end with all perseverance and supplication for all the saints.*

The word *supplication* means, "to ask or beg for humbly by earnest prayer." The word *persevere* means, "to persist in any purpose, to strive in spite of difficulties."

1 Thessalonians 5:17-18 is another passage encouraging consistent prayer:

> *Pray without ceasing, in everything give thanks; for this is the will of God in Christ Jesus for you.*

We also see consistent prayer in the life of Jesus, who spent a great amount of time in prayer. According to the Gospels, Jesus habitually rose early in the morning, often before daybreak, to commune and spend time with His Father, as we can read about in Mark 1:35:

> *Now in the morning, having risen a long while before daylight, He went out and departed to a solitary place; and there He prayed.*

Some of us have learned to diligently read and to study His Word and to set aside time for that purpose. Now we will find the same urgency for meeting God in prayer. We may think that prayer, praise, meditation, reading, and studying all have the same purpose. Of course, it is the same purpose in the broad sense of drawing near to God, but there is a difference, as Jesus points out in Luke 21:36 regarding prayer:

*Watch therefore, and **pray always** that you may be **counted worthy** to **escape** all these things that will come to pass, and to **stand** before the Son of Man.*

Jesus practiced what He taught. Jesus frequently went to the Mount of Olives or some other quiet and undisturbed place, usually alone. He went not only in the morning but also in the evening. If He needed to do it, then we certainly do also.

INTIMACY IS PERSONAL AND PRIVATE

We are in this study mainly to focus on our personal prayer life, so first let us learn from Jesus as He teaches us in Matthew 6:6:

But you, when you pray, go into your room, and when you have shut your door, pray to your Father.

We go to a private place and shut the door because we want to create a situation that is private, so we can become personal and intimate with our Father. That is easy to understand and makes a lot of sense. The question is, do we make it a reality and put it into practice? It does take some doing in order to make us available not only now and then but also on a regular basis. That is what is going to make the difference.

To prepare ourselves and make ourselves available to our Lord we even have to downplay our role as husband and wife. That might sounds a little strange, but let the word in 1 Corinthians 7:5 speak to us in this issue:

Do not deprive one another except with consent for a time, that you may give yourselves to fasting and prayer; and come together again so that Satan does not tempt you because of your lack of self-control.

So by understanding and agreement between wife and husband we give each other the freedom for privacy in personal prayer time. Of course, that does not mean that a prayer life together should become less important.

There is time for corporate prayer and Acts 1:14 is a good example of how to be in one accord in prayer:

These all continued with one accord in prayer and supplication, with the women and Mary the mother of Jesus, and with His brothers.

There are many different kinds of prayer - praying in public, prayers of dedication, and many other kinds. But now we are dealing with our personal prayer-life, so let us continue. We will conclude this introduction with a good suggestion; to remember that intimacy is personal and requires development, to be engaged in action that leads to a lasting result. To get started in that direction we need to be guided by the Holy Spirit constantly.

"OUR FATHER"

Prayer begins and ends with a main purpose: **to glorify God the Father and His Son Jesus Christ.** The purpose is not to satisfy my needs and wants. Prayer should honor the Father and downplay my role. He is the focal point, not me and my agenda. God knows everything about me anyway. We should primarily be concerned with WHO God is, WHAT He wants, and HOW we can glorify Him. That will extend His kingdom and give glory to His name. We want to bring out the very character of the Father, to block out the fulfillment of our own selfish desires and to delight in Him. In Matthew 6:32-33, Jesus very plainly taught this principle:

For after all these things the Gentiles seek. For your heavenly Father knows that you need all these things. But seek first the kingdom of God and His righteousness, and all these things shall be added to you.

Again in Matthew 6:7-8:

And when you pray, do not use vain repetitions as the heathen do. For they think that they will be heard for their many words. Therefore do not be like them. For your Father knows the things you have need of before you ask Him.

These Scripture makes it clear to us that prayer is really about glorifying our Father and not about ourselves.

Our actions have to come from our heart, and this is serious matter. Let us be aware, because we are a royal priest to our Father in heaven according to Revelation 1:6:

And has made us kings and priests to His God and Father, to Him be glory and dominion forever and ever. Amen.

And in Malachi 2:1-2 we will understand the importance God sets on this matter:

*And now, O priests, this commandment is for you. If you will not hear, and if you will not **take it to heart**, to give glory to My name," says the LORD of hosts, "I will send a curse upon you, and I will curse your blessings. Yes, I have cursed them already, because you **do not take it to heart**.*

We must realize the importance of what God teaches us here. We see that saying some words that are only our opinion about prayer casually through the day or just before we go to sleep is not going to be sufficient any more. By seeking God's Word and direction by the leading of the Holy Spirit, we will renew our mind and be transformed. To help us understand let us go to Hebrews 12:9-10:

Furthermore, we have had human fathers who corrected us, and we paid them respect. Shall we not much more readily be in subjection to the Father of spirits and live? For they indeed for a few days chastened us as seemed best to them, but He for our profit, that we may be partakers of His holiness.

Let us take a stand. We must make some changes in our lifestyle, receive the courage to be in subjection. Because the Lord is our helper, we have nothing to fear. When we arrive at that conclusion we can start to concentrate on our main purpose in prayer: TO GLORIFY OUR FATHER IN PRIVATE, INTI-MATE AND PERSONAL HEARTFELT PRAYER.

There is a very good way to do it. Start by thinking that by the Holy Spirit, we will offer the sacrifice of praise to God our Father, which is the fruit of our lips, giving thanks to His name. Yes, that sounds right and Scriptural but what if we don't know how? That is why we are studying the Word to teach us how and Hosea 14:2 has a very good suggestion:

Take words with you, and return to the LORD. Say to Him, "Take away all iniquity; receive us graciously, for we will offer the sacrifices of our lips."

The ancient Hebrew words here about sacrifice literally mean to "render the calves of our lips."

What does it mean to **take words with you**? It means that we can bring words, holy words from God's Word into our prayer. We are allowed to have a manuscript or some notes taken from the Bible. These words are to be used in guiding our thoughts and mind when we come before Him. We want to form words that express the Holy Spirit within us and so we are able to glorify our Father and God according to **His will** and our heart's desire.

*Do not fear, little flock, for it is **your Father's good pleasure** to give you the kingdom.* (Luke 12:32)

We do have to watch that it does not only become lip service, without our heart being involved or just a matter of reading words. As Jesus taught us about prayer: "do not use vain rep-etitions as the heathen. For they think that they will be heard for their many words." Our intention is to focus on Him, to give to Him our self and to continue on doing that until we are so consumed and saturated with Him - the Word Jesus Christ - that we don't need a note or a manuscript any longer. We will be flowing with living water, the Word.

This is what happens to us: we are being transformed by the renewing of our mind. We are reaching some maturity as a result of being led in the perfect will of God. We have to admit that this is our desire, so let us receive encouragement from Psalm 51:15-17:

O Lord, open my lips, and my mouth shall show forth Your praise. For You do not desire sacrifice, or else I would give it; You do not delight in burnt offering. The sacrifices of God are a broken spirit, a broken and a contrite heart; these, O God, You will not despise.

The word *contrite* means "remorseful, repentant, regretful, sorry."

SOME EXAMPLES IN PRAYER FROM MEN OF GOD

DANIEL

Daniel faced many difficult and dangerous situations, so his need for God's help and intervention must have been constant. As the Scripture teaches us, Daniel prayed by affirming the nature and character of God as we read in the book of Daniel 9:4, 9:7, and 9:9:

*And I prayed to the LORD my God, and made confession, and said, "O Lord, **great and awesome God,** who keeps His **covenant** and **mercy with** those who love Him, and with those who keep His commandments . . . O Lord, **righteous-ness belongs to You** . . . to the Lord our God belong **mercy and forgiveness**, though we have rebelled against Him."*

JONAH

Jonah is another man of God that seemed to have good cause to demand God's attention - after all, he wanted to get out of the fish. Instead Jonah extolled and praised the character of the Lord God. We know God took care of Jonah by letting

Him out. This is how he prayed in Jonah 2:7 and 2:9-10:

"When my soul fainted within me, I remembered the Lord*; and my prayer went up to You, into Your holy temple. **But I will sacrifice to You with the voice of thanksgiving**; I will pay what I have vowed* (promised). *Salvation is of the* Lord.*" So the* Lord *spoke to the fish, and it vomited Jonah onto dry land.*

PAUL AND SILAS

From the New Testament we will read about Paul and Silas. They were beaten with rods and had many stripes laid on them by the magistrates. Then they were thrown in to an inner prison and had their feet fastened in the stocks. They certainly had reason to be depressed and full of defeat, begging God to set them free. Instead as we read from Acts 16:25:

But at midnight Paul and Silas were praying and singing hymns to God, and the prisoners were listening to them.

The Bible does not tell us that Paul and Silas cried for help in their situation. God our Father was definitely glorified through all that happened and especially because God was magnified through adoration. We don't need to tell our Father what to do. Our need is to glorify and adore Him as it says in Isaiah 43:21:

This people I have formed for Myself; they shall declare My praise.

Let us read what happen that night from Acts 16:26-35:

Suddenly there was a great earthquake, so that the foundations of the prison were shaken; and immediately all the doors were opened and everyone's chains were loosed. And the keeper of the prison, awaking from sleep and seeing the prison doors open, supposing the prisoners had fled, drew his sword and was about to kill himself. But Paul called with a loud voice, saying, "Do yourself no harm, for we are all here." Then he called for a light, ran in, and fell down   trembling before Paul and Silas. And he brought them out and said, "Sirs, what must I do to be saved?" So they said, "Believe on the Lord Jesus Christ, and you will be saved, you and your household." Then they spoke the word of the Lord to him and to all who were in his house. And he took them the same hour of the night and washed their stripes. And immediately he and all his family were baptized. Now when he had brought them into his house, he set food before them; and he rejoiced, having believed in God with all his household. And when it was day, the magistrates sent the officers, saying, "Let those men go."

It is appropriate to say that this lesson does not mean that we can not ask things of our Father or bring our petition to Him. In fact we ought to according to the Word. It is the proportion, the balance we need and definitively we should not neglect to be corrected from His teaching in this subject of personal prayer life. To be more specific, the attitude we should have when we come before Him is the important lesson here. So let us pay attention when Jesus says, **"pray, then, in this way."**

In fewer than 70 words He set the pattern. It is, of course, a masterpiece of the infinite mind of God, a pattern for the structure of our own prayers. As mentioned before, Jesus did warn us of the danger of meaningless repetition.

We should regard Jesus as the one who knows best and use His guidance for our prayers, petitions, and praise - after all He is our Teacher and Master. Of course His Word is perfect and we should know the words of this prayer, but even more the spirit and attitude of that divine pattern which is only attained through the Holy Spirit's leading as we yield to Him.

So we begin with **"Our Father."** That definitely expresses a relationship between a father and a child. We must keep our focus on God and His person, so we express total and absolute dependence on Him by recognizing Him as our Father. We can address Him with so many other names but unless we know Him as our Father and consequently call Him so, we have some relationship-work with Him that needs to be done right now. Jesus used this mainly because of the great significance of the true and genuine meaning. A substitute for the real name "Father" would indicate a relationship that wasn't as intimate. This is a form that even a child can understand. Remember when Jesus said in Matthew 18:3:

Assuredly, I say to you, unless you are converted and become as little children, you will by no means enter the kingdom of heaven.

Still the most mature believer cannot fully comprehend that God is our Father, the one who gave us life and who loves, cares, provides, and protects us. The fact is that Jesus used that phrase often when He prayed or mentioned God our Father.

There is hope in your future, says the Lord, that your children shall come back to their own border.

What a promise of hope! God is our Father and He will take care of our future, He will love us, protect us and sustain us constantly. The Lord is my helper.

Hebrew 13:5 says,

Be content with such things as you have. For He Himself has said, "I will never leave you nor forsake you."

All our needs are satisfied in the intimate relationship with our Father. Our heart will be established with His grace.

"Our Father" defeats selfishness because it expresses that we are all fellow children in the household of our Father. Our prayer should embrace the whole family of faith. Ephesians 6:18 says,

Praying always with all prayer and supplication in the Spirit, being watchful to this end with all perseverance and supplication for all the saints.

We should pray what is best for all, not just for ourselves. We should do for others what we want them to do for us because our Father loves us all, and we belong to the same family. We are brothers and sisters.

GOD IS OUR FATHER

We are going to start this section with a question: is there one spiritual family of mankind under one universal fatherhood of God? Let us read some Scripture that gives us the light in this issue. First, Galatians 3:22 and 4:6:

But the Scripture has confined all under sin, that the promise by faith in Jesus Christ might be given to those who believe . . . And because you are sons, God has sent forth the Spirit of His Son into your hearts, crying out, "Abba, Father!"

We understand that only "born again" believers according to the word of God are children in His family. The Bible makes it perfectly clear that God is the Father of unbelievers only in the sense that He created them. Whoever does not abide in God the Father has another father. When Jesus spoke to the Jewish leaders (the "pastors" of that day) who opposed Him, He said in John 8:44:

You are of your father the devil, and the desires of your father you want to do. He was a murderer from the beginning, and does not stand in the truth, because there is no truth in him. When he speaks a lie, he speaks from his own resources, for he is a liar and the father of it.

In 1 John 3:9-10 we get a clear picture of this idea:

Whoever has been born of God does not sin, for His seed remains in him; and he cannot sin, because he has been born of God. In this the children of God and the children of the devil are manifest: Whoever does not practice righteousness is not of God, nor is he who does not love his brother.

The answer to the question we started with is that there is simply not just one spiritual family of mankind, under one universal Fatherhood of God. In 2 Peter 1:4 it says that only those who believe have been made partakers of the divine nature and again in John 1:12-13 it is only to those that receive Him:

*To them He gave the right to **become children of God**, to those who believe in His name: who were born, not of blood, nor of the will of the flesh, nor of the will of man, **but of God**.*

This is why we boldly can call Him our Father, being His beloved adopted children, according to the good pleasure of His will through Jesus Christ. This is the attitude and character that belongs in true prayer and the foundation for that intimate relation.

In Isaiah 64:8 we will understand how to submit to God:

But now, O LORD, You are our Father; we are the clay, and You our potter; and all we are the work of Your hand.

And so we will look to Deuteronomy 32:6 and be assured:

*Do you thus deal with the LORD, O foolish and unwise people? Is He not **your Father**, who bought you? **Has He not made you and established you**?*

CONCLUSION OF PART ONE

Once we get beyond the realm of our immediate struggles and seek God for what we need whether it is peace, fellowship, knowledge, victory, boldness, or just an understanding of what is going on then we know that our Father has an abundant supply in heavenly places. Our Father has already given it to us according to His Word and all the resources of heaven are available to us when we trust Him as our Father, who is the "true promise keeper." In Ephesians 1:3 we are assured:

*Blessed be the God and Father of our Lord Jesus Christ, who has blessed us with **every spiritual blessing** in the heavenly places in Christ.*

So what are we waiting for? Are we really benefiting from all those blessings? Of course we are, even though at times our attitude hinders our victories.

Our earthly father expected obedience and so does our heavenly Father. We remember that when Jesus, God's true Son, came down from heaven it was not to do His own will but the will of His Father. How much more are we as adopted children to be obedient and to do His will? Obedience is one of the supreme marks of our relationship with our Father and rebellion is the opposite. It is the "killer" of relations. When rebellion rules our behavior it will be evident in either our actions or reactions. There is only one remedy: repentance and asking for forgiveness, and then to show forth the fruit of repentance.

Yet in His grace our Father loves and cares for us, His own children, even when we are disobedient. In Luke 15:11-32 Jesus tells about a loving father who helps us understand how our heavenly Father reacts towards us. The father in the parable forgave and rejoiced over a self-righteous son who remained moral and upright, and also over a rebellious son who became dissolute and wandered away but then returned and repented. It is a great lesson of a compassionate father.

When we call upon **"our Father who art in heaven"** we can now do it as a child, knowing that our Father loves us and that He longs to listen to us. By these words we indicate or express our eagerness to receive His Fatherly care and blessing in any area - or better yet, all areas of our life.

His purpose as our Father is eternal, definite, and everlasting. Let us conclude with the following words from Ephesians 5:20:

*Giving thanks always for all things **to God the Father** in the name of our Lord Jesus Christ.*

Lessons in Prayer - Part Two
"HALLOWED BE THY NAME"

Here is another area where we need to understand and renew our mind, because it touches on the reason we are created: to glorify our Father in heaven and exalt His name from our hearts. The idea behind the phrase "Hallowed be Thy name" deals with this. Isaiah 43:21 explains it in a wonderful, plain way:

> *This people I have formed for Myself;*
> ***they shall declare** My praise.*

Our love and trust in our Father is not based on His names or titles but on the reality behind those names, on His very person and character. Like David the King expressed in Psalm 9:10 and 8:9:

> *And those who know Your name will put their trust in You;*
> *for You, LORD, have not forsaken those who seek You.*

> *O LORD, our Lord, how excellent is Your name*
> *in all the earth!*

We can see how God's name is esteemed in His faithfulness and truth in Isaiah 25:1:

> *O LORD, You are my God. I will exalt You, I will praise Your name, for You have done wonderful things; Your counsels of old are **faithfulness and truth**.*

When Moses went up on Mount Sinai to receive the commandments for the second time he called on the name of the Lord. Then the Lord passed by in front of Moses and proclaimed:

> *The LORD, the LORD God, merciful and gracious,*
> *long-suffering, and abounding in goodness and truth.*
> (Exodus 34:6)

So when God makes a statement like that we pay attention. Those five excellent character traits in His person are just the beginning. Let us discover how Jesus dealt with this issue as we read from John 17:6:

*I have **manifested Your name** to the men whom You have given Me out of the world. They were Yours, You gave them to Me, and they have kept Your word.*

Jesus revealed God's character to them. He did not simply give lectures on what the name meant but as He said, He manifested God to the disciples and to the whole world through His own righteous living as it says in John 1:14:

And the Word became flesh and dwelt among us, and we beheld His glory, the glory as of the only begotten of the Father, full of grace and truth.

The great commission that Jesus had to accomplish was connected with glorifying God and manifesting His name, as we can read from John 17:4 and 17:6:

I have glorified You *on the earth. I have finished the work which You have given Me to do . . .* ***I have manifested Your name*** *to the men whom You have given Me out of the world. They were Yours, You gave them to Me, and they have kept Your word.*

By living a life in the likeness of Jesus we manifest His character and apply His Word to our thinking, speaking, and acting and we are able to "hallow" God's name in our prayer. If we do not know the words or remember God's character when we approach Him in prayer, we have the great opportunity to use the principle in Hosea 14:2

Take words with you*, and return to the L*ORD*. Say to Him, "Take away all iniquity; receive us graciously, for we will offer the sacrifices of our lips."*

Let us take a look at the many different facets of His character and its expressions:

ELOHIM	The Creator God
EL ELYON	Possessor of Heaven and Earth
JEHOVAH JIREH	The LORD our Provider
JEHOVAH-NISSI	The LORD our Banner
JEHOVAH-RAPHA	The LORD that Heals
JEHOVAH-SHALOM	The LORD our Peace
JEHOVAH-RAAH	The LORD our Shepherd
JEHOVAH-TSIDKENU	The LORD our Righteousness
JEHOVAH-SABAOTH	The LORD of Hosts
JEHOVAH-SHAMA	The LORD is Present
JEHOVAH-MAGODESHKIM	The LORD Who Sanctifies Thee

To remember all those names and the meaning of them will take some effort, but if we use them often in our prayer they will become so much part of our vocabulary that they will become the expression of our heart. From Psalm 8:1 and 9:2 we will understand as we read:

*O LORD, our Lord, how excellent is **Your name** in all the earth, who have set Your glory above the heavens!*

*I will be glad and rejoice in You; I will sing praise to **Your name**, O Most High.*

Let us now take a look at the perfect manifestation of God's name as we see it in Jesus' life here on earth:

THE WAY, THE TRUTH, AND THE LIFE (John 14:6)

THE BREAD OF LIFE (John 6:35)

THE LIVING WATER (John 4:10)

THE RESURRECTION (John 11:25)

THE GOOD SHEPHERD (John 10:11)

THE LAMB OF GOD (John 1:29)

THE BRIGHT & MORNING STAR (Revelation 22:16)

THE SON OF MAN (John 1:51)

THE SON OF GOD (John 2:18)
THE LIGHT OF THE WORLD (John 8:12)
THE DOOR (John 10:9)
THE TEACHER AND THE LORD (John 13:13)
THE TRUE VINE (John 15:1)
THE KING (John 18:37)

The list is long. There are several names of God our Father and of Jesus Christ in the Old Testament. Each name speaks of His nature. For example in Isaiah 9:6 we read:

*For unto us a Child is born, unto us a Son is given; and the government will be upon His shoulder. And His name will be called **Wonderful, Counselor, Mighty God, Everlasting Father, Prince of Peace**.*

GOD'S WILL BEGINS IN THE HEART

Hallowing God's name, like every other manifestation of righteousness, begins in the heart. Like it says in 1 Peter 3:15:

But sanctify the Lord God in your hearts, *and always be ready to give a defense to everyone who asks you a reason for the hope that is in you, with meekness and fear.*

And so we are called to act according to our calling, which is stated so clearly in 1 Peter 1:15-16:

But as He who called you is holy, you also be holy in all your conduct, because it is written, "Be holy, for I am holy."

"HALLOW"

The word "hallow" is actually an archaic English word used to translate a form of the ancient Greek word *hagiazo* which means "to make holy." Words from the same ancient Greek root are translated *holy, saint, sanctify*, and *sanctification*. Be aware of how the following verses show that the sanctification process is both part of our doing and performance as well as God's promise to do His part. From Leviticus 20:7-8:

Consecrate (set apart) *yourselves therefore, and be holy, for I am the LORD your God. And you shall keep My statutes, and perform them: I am the LORD who sanctifies you.*

Again our part in sanctification can not be neglected, as we read on from 2 Corinthians 7:1:

Therefore, having these promises, beloved, let us cleanse ourselves from all filthiness of the flesh and spirit, perfecting holiness in the fear of God.

And so we go on to be completed by Him as a whole being - spirit, soul, and body - because He is faithful. We will find this idea in 1 Thessalonians 5:23-24:

Now may the God of peace Himself sanctify you completely; and may your whole spirit, soul, and body be preserved blameless at the coming of our Lord Jesus Christ. He who calls you is faithful, who also will do it.

Now we understand that these verses clearly teach us that in order to be "holy" it will take some doing of our own, but our Father and God will sanctify us completely. We do need Him don't we? So we apply this truth to our life because we know how to "hallow" His name, by obedience, reverence, honor, and by sanctification.

FAILURE TO RECOGNIZE GOD WITH HONOR AND REVERENCE

We must constantly keep in mind that the most central truth about God our Father is that He is Holy. In Isaiah 6:3 we read:

And one cried to another and said: "Holy, holy, holy is the LORD of hosts; the whole earth is full of His glory!"

When we dishonor God, the consequences can be devastating,

and we can do it in more than one way. Let us take a look at what the Word teaches us in that area.

From Numbers 20:1-12 we read about one of God's greatest servants - Moses - who stole some of the glory from God and failed to recognize and obey. God said:

*Because you did not believe Me, **to hallow Me** in the eyes of the children of Israel, therefore you shall not bring this assembly into the land which I have given them.*

We know the consequences that followed. Moses was not allowed to enter the Promised Land as a punishment for his behavior at this particular instance.

The next example is taken from Leviticus 10:1-4. There it tells us about Aaron's sons and how they offered profane fire before the Lord, which the Lord did not command them to do. Terrible consequences followed. Fire went out from the Lord and devoured them and they died before the Lord.

They offered *profane fire*, and there are a number of explanations of what that was. The fire on the altar of burnt offering was never to go out (Leviticus 6:12-13), implying that it was holy. It is possible that Nadab and Abihu brought coals of fire to the altar from a wrong source, making the sacrifice unholy. Maybe it was done at the wrong time. Whatever explanation is correct, the point is that they had been instructed what to do and how to do it, and in spite of that they did something that they were not instructed or commanded to do. It was a flagrant act of disrespect to God who had just spoke to them precisely how they were to conduct worship.

It is so easy for us to grow careless about obeying Him, to do things in our own way, to stay within our comfort zone. When we consciously and carelessly disregard His will in our life we place ourselves in a dangerous situation because we can be assured that consequences will follow, and then it is difficult to sort things out.

TO HALLOW HIS NAME . . .

It is first when we know and are able to sanctify Him in our hearts that we can transform holiness to our lives and so make sure God is hallowed in our prayer life also. To pursue perfect holiness we need to cleanse ourselves both in the flesh and in the spirit constantly and do it in the fear of God. We might have to make more effort in some areas of our life but as the Scriptures say, **"be holy yourselves in all your behavior"** (conduct). By drawing near to Him we will get to know what to do because His presence produces the truth about ourselves. Then we can show forth the fruit of repentance, cleanse our self, receive forgiveness, and become holy like He is holy.

To hallow His name is to have true knowledge of His will and who He is. To obtain the truth about God demonstrates reverence and a living, active faith. Irreverence is the opposite of hallowing His name and becomes evident when a person willingly ignores the Word of God or believes in the wrong doctrine. We could think a thought about God that is not true, or we may doubt Him, disbelieve Him and question Him. We also fail to hallow His name when we show no interest or turn away. Hebrew 11:6 says,

*But without faith it is impossible to please Him, for he who comes to **God must believe that He is**, and that He is a rewarder of those **who diligently seek Him**.*

Before we leave this area of irreverence (which actually stands in the way when we are trying to hallow His name) let us consider that some people bring ideas into their concept of God that have no place, sometimes accusing God unjustly. When we do this, we take the name of the Lord God our Father in vain. Sometimes we say things like, "God did not do that" or "God did that in my life," when the fact is that God had nothing to do with the situation whatsoever.

Even Job fell in to accusatory sin when he said, as it is recorded in the book of Job 30:21-22:

103

*But You have become cruel to me; with the strength of Your hand You oppose me. You lift me up to the wind and cause me to ride on it; **You spoil my success**.*

It is impossible to revere God and to hallow His name if we don't know His character or His will or if we do not draw near to Him continuously as a way of living. To just say, "I did not know that" is not an answer that will apply here. Lack of knowledge or rejection of knowledge will ultimately bring rejection from God.

We will get confirmation for that statement in Hosea 4:6:

*My people are destroyed for **lack of knowledge**. Because you have **rejected knowledge**, I also will reject you from being priest for Me; because you have forgotten the law of your God, I also will forget your children.*

This is serious, and we may not have been aware of this danger before, so it is important to receive knowledge and be transformed. Our Father's name is hallowed when we behave in a way that conforms to His will. When we disobey God our Father there is no room for us to hallow His name. We will diminish our capacity to revere Him. That is why we need the Holy Spirit to lead and direct us to repentance and cleansing in order to renew our mind. We do live in a time when respect and honor at large is diminishing from our lifestyle so we should not be conformed to that kind of attitude. Let us receive encouragement from the Word in Romans 3:24-25:

Being justified freely by His grace through the redemption that is in Christ Jesus, whom God set forth as a propitiation by His blood, through faith, to demonstrate His righteousness, because in His forbearance God had passed over the sins that were previously committed.

So when we approach our Father in prayer and when we have the right thoughts about Him and live righteously, we can say and proclaim **"Hallowed be Thy name"** because we know Him. Furthermore when we consciously draw Him into every daily thought, word, and activity, we will truly hallow God's name. We will focus on God like David did as we can read in Psalm 16:8 and 39:1:

I said, "I will guard my ways, lest I sin with my tongue"

I have the Lord always before me.

"Continually" is another word we can use for *always*. When we consider what those words really mean, we come to the conclusion that they describe a lifestyle. This means being aware of His presence, walking in the Spirit, and becoming anointed.

We are still focusing on prayer - to honor and hallow our God and Father even when it might seem to turn into praise. The next time we use this term "hallowed be Thy name" we are able to really approach Him with reverence, honor, and respect that is due His most holy name.

Examples of Prayer by Recognizing and Calling on the Name of God Regularly, on a Daily Basis

- Blessed are You Father of my Lord Jesus Christ in Whose name I pray. I will look up, lift my hands, take words with me and boldly come before You in spirit and in truth, through the blood of Jesus. Let my prayer be set before You as incense, that You will be pleased and receive honor, and glory. Your mighty name is excellent, I will praise You O Lord with my whole heart.

- Hallowed be Your name, Your kingdom come, Your will be done, according to Your direction. Do not lead me into testings, but deliver me from the evil one. *Jehovah Shama*, the Lord is present. You are present through Your Holy Spirit that resides in me, yes I am sealed with the Holy Spirit of promise. Your lovingkindness is better than life for You are the God of my salvation.

- Thank You *Elohim*, my Creator God; in Your presence is fullness of joy, create in me a clean heart O God and renew a right spirit within me. I bless You and rejoice because I do put all my trust in Your name. You O Lord are the portion of my inheritance. You maintain my lot; yes, I have a good inheritance. *El Elyon*, God the possessor of everything both in heaven and earth.

- *Jehovah Nissi*, the Lord my banner; let me praise You and call upon Your name, and give to You the glory due to Your name, let me also exalt Your glorious mighty name now and forever. You are the Bread of Life, the Word, the Bright and Morning Star, the Light of the World, there is nothing that I desire that compares with You. The Son of God, that became Son of Man to make me Your adopted child and made me a king and priest.

- Let me continually offer the sacrifice of praise to You God, which is the fruit of mine lips the, words that I speak out, giving thanks to Your holy name. You are the fullness, who fills all in us all. *Jehovah Jireh*, the Lord that will provide, who fulfills all my needs, I praise You Lord, You are the Good Shepherd, Everlasting Father God, receive my blessings the sacrifices of my lips, because I love You.

- Now to the King eternal, immortal, invisible; to You God who alone is wise, be honor and glory forever and ever. My soul shall be joyful in You my God, for You have clothed me with the garment of salvation, and You have covered me with the robe of righteousness, *Jehovah Tsidkenu*, the Lord my Righteousness. Lead me in Your righteousness.

- You have given me, Your own child, redemption through the blood of Jesus, and through that blood You have washed me from all my sins. You have commanded Your covenant forever; holy and awesome is Your name *Jehovah Sabaoth*, the Lord of Hosts my God, my strength, my shield and my stronghold, who is worthy to be praised, so shall I be saved from my enemies.

- Jesus the Way, the Truth and the Life. Direct me to walk that Way, teach me to speak that Truth, and guide me to live that Life, to the praise of the glory of Your grace by which You has made me accepted in the Beloved. Because I know Your name, and what the exceeding greatness of Your power is toward me who believes according to the working of Your mighty power.

- I will draw near to You with a true and pure heart, for You my Father and God have not forsaken me who seeks You. You forgive all my sins and heal all my diseases. Your name is *Jehovah Rapha*, the Lord that Healeth. Jesus the Prince of Peace, my lips shall praise You giving thanks to Your name. *Jehovah Shalom*, the Lord my Peace, You ransom me from death and surround me with love and mercies. My heart shall rejoice in Your salvation.

- *Jehovah Raah*, the Lord my Shepherd, I thank You and I praise Your glorious holy name, You will show me the path of life, and lead me to victory in Christ. Your lovingkindness is better than life. I need You Jesus the Living Water; You are the Rock of my strength, You are my defense, because You are *Jehovah Magodeskim*, the Lord that Sanctified me. You are exalted as Head over us all.

- Thank You, my Father and God, I count on You to continue to reveal, strengthen and confirm Your name in my life through the Holy Spirit, because Your name is above all names in heaven and earth. That You will anoint me with the spirit of wisdom and revelation in the knowledge of Yourself, so that I can obey from my humble and contrite heart to be submitted and dedicated to the cause of glorifying You with all what I do think and say, today and forever.

- I will fulfill my promises to You, O God, and offer a sacrifice of thanks for Your help. For You have rescued me from death; You have kept my feet from slipping. So now I can walk in Your presence, O God, in Your life-giving light. Jesus You are the Light of the World. Walk with me and talk with me. You are the resurrection. Grant me to continually glorify and uplift Your holy name.

- In everything I give thanks; for this is Your will God in Christ Jesus for me. I will not quench the Spirit, not despise prophecies; I will test all things and hold fast what is good, and I will abstain from every form of evil. I know Your name *Jehovah Magodeskim*, my Lord that sanctified me completely so that my whole spirit, soul, and body be preserved blameless at your coming.

- Now I am putting on the sturdy belt of truth, the body armor of Your righteousness. For shoes I put the peace that comes from the Good News, so that I can be fully prepared. In every battle I use faith as my shield to stop the fiery arrows aimed at me by Satan. So I put on salvation as my helmet and take up the sword of the Spirit, which is the word of God.

- I believe that You will do according to Your Word Father, exceedingly, abundantly, above all I can ask or even think according to the power that works in me, the same power that raised Jesus Christ from the dead. So through the Holy Spirit I will add faith, which is the substance of things that I am hoping for, actually the things that I can not yet see in the natural so my mind is set on things above on things that matters eternally. Amen and amen . . .

And whatever you ask in My name, that I will do, that the Father may be glorified in the Son. If you ask anything in My name, I will do it. If you love Me, keep My commandments. (John 14:13-15)

Prayer is that tool or instrument that will move the hand of God, but a tool must be used according to its maker's directions, or it will not perform well. We can recognize two of the main battle areas when we pray: one is wandering thoughts, and the second one is poor intimacy with God's character or name as revealed in His Word. Neither can be cured at once, but by submitted perseverance through discipline and obedience, initiated in our hearts delight, the cure will be evident in our life, and pleasing to *Elohim* our Creator God.

We delight to be transformed by doing His will!

Lessons in Prayer - Part Three
"THY KINGDOM COME"

Our Father in heaven has intended for us to be a special treasure to Him, but there is a condition that we have to fulfill. The outcome of it will affect the rest of the people around us as well as our self. To be that kind of treasure or priests we need to understand that we definitely must renew our mind in this area as well. Let us be open for the Holy Spirit's leading, and receive from the Word of God in Exodus 19:5-6:

> *"Now therefore, if you will indeed obey My voice and keep My covenant, then you shall be a special treasure to Me above all people; for all the earth is Mine. And you shall be to Me a kingdom of priests and a holy nation." These are the words which you shall speak to the children of Israel.*

There are several Scriptures that establish the same ideas, such as Deuteronomy 7:6, 14:21, and 26:19 just to mention some of them. In the New Covenant we are the children of God. To confirm that, let us read from the New Testament:

> *Having predestined us to adoption as sons by Jesus Christ to Himself, according to the good pleasure of His will.*
> (Ephesians 1:5)

> *You also, as living stones, are being built up a spiritual house, a holy priesthood, to offer up spiritual sacrifices acceptable to God through Jesus Christ.* (1 Peter 2:5)

So this is the kind of people that God has in mind for us to be: a holy priesthood - as individuals, as a church, and as a nation. He wants us to be a part of His Kingdom, and to pray **"THY KINGDOM COME."**

- **We** His special treasure
- **We** His kingdom of Priests

111

- **We** the living stones, His spiritual temple
- **We, HIS KINGDOM**

This is not only talking about the clergy, but all of us who believe.

OUR PRESENT SITUATION!

"YOUR KINGDOM COME" means that we are that kingdom of priests, who are bringing the Kingdom of God to the rest of the world. By the Holy Spirit we are able to accomplish this amazing task. Sometimes, somehow, are we mixing His Kingdom with the kingdom of this world? We deceive the world and ourselves by representing the wrong kingdom - the world system - by the way we live and conduct ourselves.

If we look at ourselves and our values - regardless in what situation we are - in view of the word of God and being honest we might disqualify ourselves by the way we mix in this world's values with His values. James 4:4 tells us:

Adulterers and adulteresses! Do you not know that friendship with the world is enmity with God? Whoever therefore wants to be a friend of the world makes himself an enemy of God.

The kingdom of this world is constantly opposed to the Kingdom of God, so when we mix them we are disobedient and cause confusion. Jesus was very definite when He stated, **"My Kingdom is not of this world."**

Let us consider the following from Deuteronomy 28:10:

Then all peoples of the earth shall see that you are called by the name of the Lord, and they shall be afraid of you.

If the Kingdom of God were evident in our Churches, then that statement **"they shall be afraid of you,"** would be more true. At the very least, people would pay more attention to the Church, and we would surely have an impact on our society. Sadly, the facts are clear and the evidence is the opposite. Let us be honest and admit our dilemma. The same problem and controversies that exist in the world or in the community at large also exist among the people in most of our Churches. What actually characterizes the societies we live in are the almighty dollar and business as usual. These things prevail in most of our Churches as well. No human kingdom, whatever the Church name might be, or our society as a whole can ever come into agreement with God's Kingdom as long as we function apart from God's Kingdom and do not follow Biblical fundamental principles.

When we pray, **"Your Kingdom come"** it involves a completely different standard than what the kingdoms of this world stand for. The gates of Hell will never prevail against God's Kingdom. So let us not get confused by the present situation, but be grounded in the truth of the Word of God and make the difference by not conforming to the present situation.

That He would grant you, according to the riches of His glory, to be strengthened with might through His Spirit in the inner man, that Christ may dwell in your hearts through faith; that you being rooted and grounded in love.
(Ephesians 3:16-17)

WE ARE TO MAKE A DIFFERENCE!

If we are part of "GOD'S KINGDOM" then we should be a **significantly different** kind of people, unlike the rest in the world. Exodus 19:6 tells us:

You shall be to me a kingdom of priest,
a special treasure to me above all people.

Why did God choose us? Well, let's find out:

But because the LORD loves you, and because He would keep the oath which He swore to your fathers, therefore know that the LORD your God, He is God, the faithful God who keeps

covenant and mercy for a thousand generations with those **who love Him and keep His commandments.**
(Deuteronomy 7:8-9)

And of course, we know that He gave us His only Son Jesus Christ to die for our sins, in the New Covenant. What a glorious love, what a wonderful confirmation in Revelation 1:5-6:

And from Jesus Christ, the faithful witness, the firstborn from the dead, and the ruler over the kings of the earth. To Him who loved us and washed us from our sins in His own blood, and has made us kings and priests to His God and Father, to Him be glory and dominion forever and ever. Amen.

That must by all definition and interpretation mean that we **definitely should be a different kind of people**, who do not have the same kind of lifestyle as the people that do **not** belong to His Kingdom. That is why God said in Deuteronomy 5:29:

Oh, that they had such a heart in them that they would fear Me and always keep all My commandments, that it might be well with them and with their children forever!

Philippians 2:15 communicates the same idea:

That you may become blameless and harmless, children of God without fault in the midst of a crooked and perverse generation, among whom **you shine as lights in the world.**

WE ARE CREATED FOR HIM, FOR HIM ONLY

From Isaiah 43:21 we can be assured why He created us:

This people I have formed for Myself; they shall declare My praise.

So our Father in heaven has made it clear, that we His Kingdom, who are called out of darkness into His marvelous light,

114

we **shall** act according to His will in **all** areas of our life. If we don't, we display disobedience, pursuing a different kingdom. To clear out some of the obstacles that we are up against, let us go to Hebrews 3:18-19 and 4:1-2:

And to whom did He swear that they would not enter His rest, but to those who did not obey? So we see that they could not enter in because of unbelief.

Therefore, since a promise remains of entering His rest, let us fear lest any of you seem to have come short of it. For indeed the gospel was preached to us as well as to them; but the word which they heard did not profit them, not being mixed with faith in those who heard it.

Therefore, beloved partakers of the heavenly calling, this is our confession: "Thy Kingdom come."

To His Majesty,
Let my praises be,
Pure and holy, giving glory
To the King of Kings

And nothing I desire compares with You,
O Lord my God.

"Your Kingdom come," and everything that comes with it. We will welcome righteousness and peace and joy in the Holy Spirit. That means that we will become active in our duty as kings and priests. We will bring sacrifices of prayer and thanksgiving before Him. That will in turn require time to do that daily. What a glorious duty! Consider the following from Luke 9:62 and 2 Timothy 4:10:

*But Jesus said to him, "No one, having put his hand to the plow, **and looking back**, is fit for the **kingdom of God**."*

*For Demas has forsaken me, **having loved this present world**, and has departed.*

LET US DO, "YOUR KINGDOM COME"

Remember who has saved us, redeemed us and called us with a holy calling; not according to man's ways (which are many) but He called us according to His own purpose to His Kingdom. Let us hold fast the pattern of sound words, words that He spoke, and taught us to pray **"Your Kingdom come."** We should really consider what this does imply.

Since we now are confident that God has made us Kings and Priest unto Himself, to present ourselves as a holy sacrifice to glorify Him in all our actions, displaying the love for our Father that is expressed according to His will in so many places in the Bible, let us take a look at some of them, starting at Romans 12:1-2 and Matthew 6:33:

*I beseech you therefore, brethren, by the mercies of God, that you present your bodies a **living sacrifice, holy, acceptable to God**, which is your reasonable service. And **do not be conformed to this world**, but be transformed by the renewing of your mind, that you may prove what is that good and acceptable and perfect will of God.*

*But seek **first the kingdom of God** and His righteousness, and all these things shall be added to you.*

How outstandingly clear the Word is:

- **Your** kingdom come
- **Your** will be done
- For **Yours** is the kingdom
- Seek **His** righteousness

Our focus should be on **Him, Our Father**. Lay up for yourself treasures in heaven, for where your treasure is, there your heart will be also. Both this world and heaven are His domain, so we better pay attention to Him. In fact He has promised that He will take care of all our needs. In spite of all the promises and the evidence of His loving kindness, we tend to build our own kingdoms, and live based on the rules and the behavior of this world. Let us stop doing that, leave that behind, take on Him and do it His way, "**His kingdom come**." Because Jesus addressed the church and this issue in Matthew 7:21-23, it certainly is a picture of a mix between the church and the world:

*Not everyone who says to Me, "Lord, Lord," shall enter the kingdom of heaven, but he **who does the will of My Father in heaven**. Many will say to Me in that day, "Lord, Lord, have we not prophesied in Your name, cast out demons in Your name, and done many wonders in Your name?" And then I will declare to them, "I never knew you; depart from me you who practice lawlessness!"*

"LET US" MEANS AN ACTIVITY - "TO DO IT!" WHAT DOES THIS MEAN?

Whether we feel that we are ready or if we are a bit hesitant, let us get some more assurance. Since He will fill our every need, we should respond with a desire to transform our lives and spend more time in doing like it says in 2 Corinthians 7:1:

*Therefore, having these promises, beloved, **let us cleanse ourselves** from all filthiness of the flesh and spirit, **perfecting holiness** in the fear of God.*

We do understand that the term *let us* is an activity that takes some doing on our part, and again *cleansing* is another word that involves our action. If we do not know how, then we really have to find out because if the Word of God tells us to do something in order to perfect holiness and we do not know how to practically go about it, then it will be of absolutely no benefit.

So now we are ready to conclude what we have received so far about "YOUR KINGDOM COME." These are the riches of His Word; let us do what the Word has disclosed and we will receive strength to comprehend the fullness of our prayer, through the Holy Spirit.

Let us have the same heart the Apostle Paul had:

I press toward the goal for the prize of the upward call of God in Christ Jesus. Therefore let us, as many as are mature, have this mind; and if in anything you think otherwise, God will reveal even this to you.
(Philippians 3:14-15)

Lessons in Prayer - Part Four
"THY WILL BE DONE"

Let us continue to learn how to pray and especially the prayer that our Lord Jesus taught us. We have now arrived to the sentence **"Thy will be done"** on earth as it is in heaven. So when we pray, it is very clear that it has to be according to His will, or His will is to become our will as we discover in Psalm 40:8:

> *I delight to do your will, O my God,*
> *and Your law is within my heart.*

What a perfect description of a perfect situation! This is God's way, and we should embrace and accept it, making an effort and doing all we can to apply it completely. Jesus was committed to do the Father's will and that should be our attitude also. In John 4:34 and John 6:38, we notice that Jesus had to lay down His will.

> *Jesus said to them, "My food is to do **the will of Him who sent Me** and to finish His work. For I have come down from heaven, **not to do My own will, but the will of Him who sent Me**.*

We have a tendency to pray away in our ignorance and not be aware what our Father's will is in this particular area - so let us change some of our thinking and behavior. Take on an attitude to act according to His will as we discover it through His Word: **"Thy will be done."** We can prove what is the perfect will of God by the directions in Romans 12:2:

> *And do not be conformed to this world, but be transformed by the renewing of your mind, that you may **prove** what is that good and **acceptable and perfect will of God**.*

"Thy will be done." According to the good pleasure of His will we are adopted in to His family and accepted in Him by

Jesus Christ. We should never refuse to accept that marvelous goodness and love to become that kind of person, that son or daughter that He wants us to be. **"Thy will be done on earth as it is in heaven"** - yes, and we are here on earth so it has to be done in us and through the Holy Spirit's leading, teaching us to obey and follow His will, for we are His workmanship created in His image in Christ Jesus.

In everything give thanks; for this is the will of God in Christ Jesus for you. (1 Thessalonians 5:18)

*Then I said, "Behold, I have come; in the volume of the book it is written of Me; **to do Your will, O God**."* (Hebrews 10:7)

PASSIVE RESIGNATION

When we pray for His will to be done, we must be careful of passive resignation that may come just because He commands us to pray. Sometimes prayer becomes more a matter of capitulation or giving up. We might not have any more instruction or suggestions to give God in our particular situation, so we let God take over by saying "Thy will be done."

Another harmful attitude is thinking that our prayer does not make any difference and that His will be done regardless of how we pray. If this is the situation in our prayer, that will mean that we accept God's will with a defeatist attitude.

Our prayer lives become weak because we don't believe our prayers will accomplish anything significant. We should pray with confidence and belief. Even in the early church, when faith was generally prevalent, prayer could be passive and the answer unexpected. Please read Acts 12:1-16 at the end of this chapter. In the following we only quote Acts 12:5 and 12:16:

*Peter was therefore kept in prison, **but constant prayer** was offered to God for him by the church . . . Now Peter continued knocking; and when they opened the door and saw him, **they were astonished**.*

By reading the whole passage it gives us the complete message. They prayed and the answer came while they were praying, and when it became evident, they were astonished. It is a magnificent lesson.

Our attitude must express our expectation and belief, so when we know His will, it should become more evident in our prayer. The result should be an attitude of continual praise and thanksgiving, rejoicing in the Father and God who is the creator of us all and who loves us.

So when God's will is done in our prayer life, it will certainly make a difference. Let us be inspired by the following word from Hebrews 10:35-36:

*Therefore do not cast away **your confidence**, which has great reward. For you have need **of endurance**, so that after you **have done the will of God, you may receive the promise**.*

TO REPLACE OUR WILL WITH HIS WILL

- "Why can't I pray the way **I** want to?"
- "Has God not given me **my own** will?"
- "Does it **have** to be done in a certain way?"
- "I want do it my way because **God made me** this way!"
- "Why make it so **complicated**?"

If these are some of the questions we ask, then we really have to be transformed in our mind. Before we can pray for God's will to be done in our life, there has to be an attitude of willingness and openness. We have to be aware that the major obstacle is **PRIDE** and must be dealt with.

Pride caused Satan to rebel against God. Pride causes unbelievers to reject God and believers to disobey Him. Our own opinion, not based on knowledge, is the substance of our pride.

By the course of nature pride will become more prevalent in us the older we get, even to the point that we could call it being "opinionated," "stubborn" or even "ignorant." That is certainly not the way to mature in the Spirit. Acts 17:30 has the answer, so let us apply that to our life, because it is more than an answer. It is a command, not only to believers, but also to all men everywhere:

> *Truly, these times of ignorance God overlooked, but now commands all men everywhere to repent.*

To begin with, based on sincerity and faith, we have to be convinced that this is God's will for us personally. We need to abandon or plainly just get rid of our own will for God's will to completely reign in our lives in all areas. When we are convinced, the next step will be to make a commitment. Now this might become a struggle and most likely it will take form in us over a period of time. God is not in any hurry and we are all different in our set ways. Practically it is a great advantage to work through this process on a constant basis. That is why our loving Father has explained it so well in His Word, the Bible.

Until we are willing to sacrifice our will and to make our life become a living and holy sacrifice by the renewing of our mind and until our will is replaced with His will, it is clear and evident that GOD'S WILL CAN NOT BE MANIFESTED IN OUR LIFE.

God's commands demand obedience and commitment. Many other things in life do command commitment, so let us recognize it when God does command it, and accept it without murmuring and disputing.

"Thy will be done" should be relatively easy to comply with when we put our trust in Him and His endless patience with us. Why is it then, that we don't do it? The answer is simple. We resist His will by constantly exercising our own will in so many areas of our life, even now as we deal with our prayer life we would rather do it our own way.

We should not let pride become the reason for the resistance, but do as the Word says, "bear fruit worthy of repentance." We must admit our sins and so confess them on a regular basis. We should be aware so that we do not let pride keep us from admitting that our will needs to be transformed by the renewing of our mind. We should be aware so that pride does not keep us from not accepting the Holy Spirit's correction when we are confronted and convinced.

A changed will is a part of the new life and it is not a condition for our salvation, but it should be the supernatural outcome of our Father's will that expresses through faith in action with wisdom and knowledge. So from now and forever we can pray with a new and fresh insight **"THY WILL BE DONE ON EARTH AS IT IS IN HEAVEN."**

We will conclude this part with some encouraging words from Philippians 1:9-11:

> *And this I pray, that your love may abound still more and more in knowledge and all discernment, that you may approve the things that are excellent, that you may be sincere and without offense till the day of Christ, being filled with the fruits of righteousness which are by Jesus Christ, to the glory and praise of God.*

ACTS 12:1-17

> *Now about that time Herod the king stretched out his hand to harass some from the church. Then he killed James the brother of John with the sword. And because he saw that it pleased the Jews, he proceeded further to seize Peter also. Now it was during the Days of Unleavened Bread. So when he had arrested him, he put him in prison, and delivered him to four squads of soldiers to keep him, intending to bring him before the people after Passover.* **Peter was therefore kept in prison, but constant prayer was offered to God for him by the church.** *And when Herod was about to bring him out, that night Peter was sleeping, bound with two chains*

123

between two soldiers; and the guards before the door were keeping the prison.

*Now behold, an angel of the Lord stood by him, and a light shone in the prison; and he struck Peter on the side and raised him up, saying, "Arise quickly!" And his chains fell off his hands. Then the angel said to him, "Gird yourself and tie on your sandals;" and so he did. And he said to him, "Put on your garment and follow me." So he went out and followed him, and did not know that what was done by the angel was real, but thought he was seeing a vision. When they were past the first and the second guard posts, they came to the iron gate that leads to the city, which opened to them of its own accord; and they went out and went down one street, and immediately the angel departed from him. And when Peter had come to himself, he said, "Now I know for certain that the Lord has sent His angel, and has delivered me from the hand of Herod and from all the expectation of the Jewish people." So, when he had considered this, he came to the house of Mary, the mother of John whose surname was Mark, **where many were gathered together praying.** And as Peter knocked at the door of the gate, a girl named Rhoda came to answer. **When she recognized Peter's voice, because of her gladness** she did not open the gate, but ran in and announced that Peter stood before the gate. But they said to her, **"You are beside yourself!" Yet she kept insisting that it was so. So they said, "It is his angel." Now Peter continued knocking; and when they opened the door and saw him, they were astonished.***

But motioning to them with his hand to keep silent, he declared to them how the Lord had brought him out of the prison. And he said, "Go, tell these things to James and to the brethren." And he departed and went to another place.

Lessons in Prayer - Part Five
GIVE US THIS DAY OUR DAILY BREAD

We have learned so far that prayer is communication with our Father and that prayer begins and ends with the purpose of glorifying God the Father and His Son Jesus Christ, not our needs and wants. Prayer must honor the Godhead, and downplay our own role. He is the focus point, not us and not our own agenda. It might sound strange, but the fact is that that prayer can become a idol in our life if we use it to direct God and tell Him what to do and when and how to do it.

Nothing I desire compares with You . . .
Be exalted, oh Lord my God.

Prayer should primarily be concerned with who God is, what He wants, and how He can be glorified. That is exactly what Jesus taught us in the first half of the prayer.

Now we are about to move in to the next half. Here we will discover how He will sustain what He created. We remember the name **Jehovah-Jireh,** which means, **"The LORD Will Provide."** He created us for Himself:

This people I have formed for Myself; they shall declare My praise. (Isaiah 43:21)

When we pray "GIVE US THIS DAY OUR DAILY BREAD," it will bring us to a state of declaring our dependence on Him to sustain us - but notice that we are only to ask for this day and only what we need for our "daily" portion. Notice also that we pray "GIVE US" because it is not only for myself.

In Exodus 16:4 we can read that God preserved His people from hunger in the wilderness:

Then the LORD said to Moses, "Behold, I will rain bread from heaven for you. And the people shall go out and gather a certain quota every day, that I may test them, whether they will walk in My law or not."

By reading the whole chapter, we can really learn and understand the importance of this lesson about the bread. Let's continue reading from Exodus 16:16:

*This is the thing which the LORD has commanded: "Let every man gather it according **to each one's need,** one omer for each person, according to the number of persons; let every man take for those who are in his tent."*

This is a great lesson: God gave them manna to eat consistently for 40 years.

Now as the Holy Spirit makes us understand, let us go on to the New Testament and receive from Jesus teaching in John 6:31-35, John 6:47-51, and John 6:58:

*"Our fathers ate the manna in the desert; as it is written, 'He gave them bread from heaven to eat.'" Then Jesus said to them, "Most assuredly, I say to you, Moses did not give you the bread from heaven, but My Father gives you the true bread from heaven. For the bread of God is He who comes down from heaven and gives life to the world." Then they said to Him, "Lord, give us this bread always." And Jesus said to them, "**I am the bread of life**. He who comes to Me shall never hunger, and he who believes in Me shall never thirst."*

*"Most assuredly, I say to you, he who believes in Me has everlasting life. **I am the bread of life**. Your fathers ate the manna in the wilderness, and are dead. This is the **bread** which comes down from heaven, that one may eat of it and not die. **I am the living bread** which came down from heaven. If anyone eats of this **bread**, he will live forever; and the **bread** that I shall give is My flesh, which I shall give for the life of the world."*

*"This is the bread which came down from heaven; not as your fathers ate the manna, and are dead. **He who eats this bread will live forever.**"*

Just a reminder, as we started in Exodus 16 and saw that the children of Israel *murmured against Moses and Aaron, and Moses said, "your murmurings are not against us but against the Lord."* Even so our focus should be on **Jesus. He is our daily bread**, let us understand Him fully. Matthew 6:25 and 6:32 makes it even clearer:

Therefore I say to you, do not worry about your life, what you will eat or what you will drink; nor about your body, what you will put on. Is not life more than food and the body more than clothing?

For after all these things the Gentiles seek. For your heavenly Father knows that you need all these things.

This is why we should never lose our constant dependence on Him for our daily bread. Physically and spiritually we will focus on spiritual matters, and always trust that God will take care of our physical needs. Sometimes God provides for His children through miraculous means, but His primary way of provision is through work, because He will provide energy, resources, wisdom, and opportunity, as the Apostle Paul explained:

For even when we were with you, we commanded you this: If anyone will not work, neither shall he eat. For we hear that there are some who walk among you in a disorderly manner, not working at all, but are busybodies. Now those who are such we command and exhort through our Lord Jesus Christ that they work in quietness and eat their own bread.
(2 Thessalonians 3:10-12)

Because He promised to provide all our physical needs we can pray confidently and thankfully to our God and Father that He will supply the provision each day according to "GIVE US THIS DAY OUR DAILY BREAD." So that is a valid petition that comes from the Father's heart to care for His children, especially as we keep in mind Jesus is the bread of life, the living bread.

What conclusion could we now draw out of all this? If we seek Him first with a right heart, spend our effort to draw near to Him and glorify Him, then our heavenly Father will supply all our needs in all areas of our life according to His riches in heaven.

Before we end this part, let us take one more step toward understanding what God taught by His works in the desert as we read in Exodus 16, but now by reading from Psalm 78:17-19 and 78:22:

But they sinned even more against Him by rebelling against the Most High God in the wilderness. And they tested God in their heart by asking for the food of their fancy. Yes, they spoke against God: They said, "Can God prepare a table in the wilderness?"

Because they did not believe in God, and did not trust in His salvation.

As we continue on in Psalm 78:23-25:

Yet He had commanded the clouds above, and opened the doors of heaven, had rained down manna on them to eat, and given them of the bread of heaven. Men ate angels' food; He sent them food to the full. He also rained meat on them like the dust, feathered fowl like the sand of the seas; and He let them fall in the midst of their camp, all around their dwellings.

And so they had to pay the consequences of their behavior. We will find this in Psalm 78:29-31 and 78:8:

*So they ate and were well filled, **for He gave them their own desire**. They were not deprived of their craving; but while their food was still in their mouths, the wrath of God came against them, and slew the stoutest of them, and struck down the choice men of Israel.*

*And may not be like their fathers, a stubborn and rebellious generation, a generation that **did not set its heart aright**, and whose spirit was **not faithful to God**.*

When we ask God to give us the desires of our heart, we must be certain that the heart is right with God before we express our desire. The Holy Spirit will guide us in all things and teach us. This is why we have to learn how to do things His way and how to pray according to His will. Our attitude should reflect a renewed mind and a repentant heart, willingly praying, **"GIVE US THIS DAY OUR DAILY BREAD."**

A right perspective of God our Father is a condition for a right relationship. To know Him is the only true assurance of eternal life. When our desire is HIM and HIM only, then there will be pleasures for evermore.

Lessons in Prayer - Part Six
"FORGIVE US OUR DEBTS, AS WE FORGIVE OUR DEBTORS"

We are now entering the part in our prayer that deals with the obstacle or hindrance to our communication with our Father - our sin, our daily sin. It is not only our communication that is hindered, but our fellowship, our whole relationship with Him is damaged, and even our earthly relations are affected because we neglect to deal with the real problem in our life - our sin.

Often we will neglect and get trapped in the symptoms of our sickness or sin while we overlook the real reason behind it, but our Father knows. So let us receive knowledge and learn how to make use of Jesus our Lord's teaching. Because we are born again believers and have been blessed with the assurance of our relationship with our Father in heaven, it does not automatically ensure that our communication is functioning properly. We maybe have experienced that situation in our relationships with other people. Sometimes our family relationships are the most difficult ones, with broken communications as a result of unforgiveness and issues that have not been dealt with properly. The consequence of this is broken and the resulting bad relationships. Prayer is our communication with our Father. Jesus teaches us in Matthew 6:14-15 about the principle in these matters:

For if you forgive men their trespasses, your heavenly Father will also forgive you. But if you do not forgive men their trespasses, neither will your Father forgive your trespasses.

Don't we all, even if we are born again believers, sin now and then? We are all sinners, so that is nothing new. Does that mean that we all have a bad relationship with God, because our sin separates us from God? To understand how to deal with this situation in a practical way let us read from Ecclesiastics 7:20 and then from 1 John 1:8-9.

For there is not a just man on earth who does
good and does not sin.

If we say that we have no sin, we deceive ourselves, and the
truth is not in us. If we confess our sins, He is faithful and
just to forgive us our sins and to cleanse us from all
unrighteousness.

That is our greatest need as believers. We need forgiveness of our sins, and we need to understand that we must deal with this on a constant and continuing basis. Sin will rob us of the fullness of life by burdening the conscience with unrelenting guilt. 1 John 3:20-21 deals with just this point:

For if our heart condemns us, God is greater than our heart,
and knows all things. Beloved, if our heart does not con-
demn us, we have confidence toward God.

The confidence to come to God with our sin, to confess and repent sounds so simple and still it is so often neglected. It is a life-giving vital part in our life that must not be neglected in our daily time before our God and Father. Confession is necessary because our sins will separate us from God and our prayer will not be heard. So let us receive this lesson and become open and willing to confess and repent and turn to that part in the prayer regarding confession and repentance and then sin no more. **"Forgive us our debts, as we forgive our debtors."**

WE NEED TO OVERCOME
OUR SINS - HOW?

Sin carries us away from God and if we follow where it carries us, it ultimately separates us completely. Without question, sin is the principal enemy and our greatest problem unless we follow God's plan of salvation. Here are three passages from the Bible that in a practical way will explain to us how:

> *I acknowledged my sin to You, and my iniquity I have not hidden. I said, "I will confess my transgressions to the LORD," and You forgave the iniquity of my sin. Selah.*
> (Psalm 32:5)

> *And everyone who has this hope in Him* **purifies himself**, *just as He is pure.* (1 John 3:3)

> *We know that whoever is born of God does not sin; but he who has been born of God* **keeps himself**, *and the wicked one does not touch him.* (1 John 5:18)

Since our most severe problem is sin, our greatest need is forgiveness and that is exactly what God our Father provides. Though we have been forgiven the ultimate penalty of sin through salvation in Jesus Christ, we are desperately in need of Him through the Holy Spirit's guidance to help us produce fruit worthy of repentance. Are we familiar with how sin is constantly working, so we can recognize it and turn from its defilement?

THE DEGENERATIVE POWER

Because our heart is wicked and deceitful, sin is the king and ruler of our heart. Do we agree with that statement as being the truth from the Word of God? Of course, because in Jeremiah 17:9 we can read:

> *The heart is deceitful above all things, and desperately wicked; who can know it?*

Sin is the first lord of the soul and it has contaminated every living being. Sin is the degenerative power in humans. Sin will show itself in disease, illness, misery, pain, sickness, death, and hell. Sin is the real reason for every broken marriage, every disrupted home, every broken friendship, every argument, every disloyalty, every hatred, and every selfishness. The list is long. Sin is the moral and spiritual disease for which man has no cure.

God has the answer. Jesus Christ His Son bore all our diseases and sicknesses and problems and nailed them to the cross, and we are free to choose His way to produce fruit worthy of repentance and live.

SIN DOMINATES OUR MIND

*Because, although **they knew God**, they did not glorify Him as God, nor were thankful, but became futile in their **thoughts**, and their foolish **hearts** were darkened.*
(Romans 1:21)

SIN DOMINATES OUR WILL

*For the good that I will to do, I do not do; but the evil **I will** not to do, that **I practice**. Now if I do what I will not to do, it is no longer I who do it, **but sin that dwells in me**.*
(Romans 7:19-20)

The Bible passages we just read explain our present situation in the flesh, and how the sin is in control if we do not take charge over our life. Sometimes we are tempted to use those passages as an excuse for our sinful behavior. As usual we must continue to read and understand the whole meaning of the context. *If we live according to the will of our flesh, we will die.* Here are two passages from the Bible that will help us to understand this dilemma:

*For if you live according to the flesh **you will die**; but if by the Spirit you put to death the deeds of the body, **you will live**.* (Romans 8:13)

For sin shall not have dominion over you, for you are not under law but under grace. (Romans 6:14)

Sin dominates the emotions, affections and the feelings. The natural man does not want his sin to be cured, because the natural man loves darkness rather than light. Consequently if we are ruled by our emotions, affections and the feelings, our deeds will be according to these rules, whether we want it that way or not. John 3:19-21 will help us to understand:

And this is the condemnation, that the light has come into the world, and men loved darkness rather than light, because their deeds were evil. For everyone practicing evil hates the light and does not come to the light, lest his deeds should be exposed. **But he who does the truth comes to the light, that his deeds may be clearly seen, that they have been done in God.**

OUR OLD CONDITION OR, WHAT WE ARE BY NATURE

By nature we resist doing what the Word of God commands us to do. When it comes to spiritual matters everything in us and in this world is opposed to that. That is why we so desperately need the Holy Spirit's constant leading. Jesus Christ died so we can enjoy deliverance from this present condition, which is the sin or this present evil world that is at work and wants to dominate us. We will understand it better by reading from Galatians 1:4 and Titus 2:14:

Who gave Himself for our sins, that He might deliver us from this present evil age, according to the will of our God and Father

Who gave Himself for us, that He might redeem us from every lawless deed and purify for Himself His own special people, zealous for good works.

When we are disobedient sin will bring us under the control of Satan. The flesh longs to keep us under the old condition, by nature it moves to fulfill our desires as children of Satan or we could say that we are guided by the prince of the power of the air, the ruler of this present evil world. In Ephesians 2:1-3, it clearly explains our situation:

> *And you He made alive, who were dead in trespasses and sins, in which you once walked according to the course of this world, according to the prince of the power of the air, the spirit who now works in the sons of disobedience, among whom also we all once conducted ourselves in the lusts of our flesh, fulfilling the desires of the flesh **and of the mind, and were by nature children of wrath, just as the others.***

Psalm 51:3 and Psalm 51:5 also confirm our situation and help us to realize that we do need our redeemer Jesus Christ:

> *For I acknowledge my transgressions, and*
> *my sin is always before me*
>
> *Behold, I was brought forth in iniquity, and*
> *in sin my mother conceived me.*

DIFFERENT MEANINGS OF THE WORD "SIN"

Forgive us our *debts*, is the word that Matthew uses. Forgive us our *sins* is the word from Luke. Are there different forms of sin and can we benefit from knowing the difference? Of course. Jesus teaches His disciples that the debts referred to here are those debts incurred by believers, not unbelievers since this prayer is a model for us. Sin is defilement, a dishonor, and a violation of His law. It is a crime that needs to be dealt with and *we owe a debt of obedience.* Consequently we have incurred a debt of punishment, a guilt that allows the enemy to carry out the punishment. We certainly need our daily physical bread, but how much more important is Jesus the bread of life, and the Holy Spirit, because we need continued forgiveness of our sin.

1. DEBT SIN

The word *debt* that Matthew uses is the ancient Greek word *opheilema* (*of-i-lay-ma*) which means, "something owed, a due, morally a fault, a debt, a person indebted, a delinquent, a transgression against God, obligation, to be bound, ought, must, should, to fail in duty." It clearly indicates that the reference is to sin, not to financial debt. Matthew probably used the term *opheilema* because it corresponds to the most common Aramaic term for sin used among the Jews in that day, a term that also represented moral or spiritual debt to God. Let's see how it is used in Matthew 6:12:

> *And forgive us our debts,* (opheilema)
> *as we forgive our debtors* (opheiletes)

2. OFFENSE SIN

The ancient Greek word *hamartia* means "offense, to miss the mark (and so not share in the prize), to err, especially morally, sin, trespass." This word for sin is most commonly used in the New Testament. So in Luke 11:4 we can read:

> *And forgive us our sins,* (hamartia) *for we also forgive everyone who is indebted* (opheilo) *to us.*

This is a good example showing how these two words both refer to sin. The difference between them, as we can see, is that *hamartia* sin has the idea of "to do something wrong," while *opheilo* sin has the idea of doing something that has to be paid back, like a debt.

3. TRESPASS SIN

The ancient Greek word *parabtoma* often refers to a "trespass" which has the meaning, "a slide-slip (a lapse or a deviation), an unintentional error, fall, fault, offense, sin, or trespass." The idea is a result more from carelessness than from intentional disobedience. Matthew uses this word in a different passage in the Bible, but he still quotes Jesus as He taught about prayer in Matthew 6:14-15:

For if you forgive men their trespasses, (parabtoma) your heavenly Father will also forgive you. But if you do not forgive men their trespasses, neither will your Father forgive your trespasses (parabtoma).

4. INIQUITY SIN

The ancient Greek word *anomia* or *anomos* means "iniquity, lawlessness, illegality, as in the violation of law, or wickedness, transgression of the law, unrighteousness, without law, lawless, unlawful, and wicked." It definitely expresses an intentional and flagrant sin. It describes a direct and open rebellion against God and His will. Let us take a look at how sin or lawlessness is described in 1 Timothy 1:9-10:

Knowing this: that the law is not made for a righteous person, but for the lawless and insubordinate, for the ungodly and for sinners, for the unholy and profane, for murderers of fathers and murderers of mothers, for manslayers, for fornicators, for sodomites, for kidnappers, for liars, for perjurers, and if there is any other thing that is contrary to sound doctrine.

So it is a description of ungodly people, mostly criminals, those who are not Christians. But we know that even so-called Christians are involved in those things, to a large extent because of the lack of boundaries in the existing Church systems. There is little or no accountability, and a lack of sound doctrine.

It is interesting to see how Matthew is using this term, from Matthew 7:23, 13:41, 23:28, and 24:12:

And then I will declare to them, "I never knew you; depart from Me, you who practice lawlessness!"(anomia)

The Son of Man will send out His angels, and they will gather out of His kingdom all things that offend, and those who practice lawlessness. (anomia)

Even so you also outwardly appear righteous to men, but inside you are full of hypocrisy and lawlessness. (anomia)

And because lawlessness (anomia) *will abound, the love of many will grow cold.*

5. TRANSGRESSION SIN

The ancient Greek word *parabaino* or *parabasis* is the fifth word in the New Testament used for sin. It is often translated "transgression." This sin is more conscious and intentional. Let us see how Strong's Concordance defines this word: "to go contrary to, violate a command, violation, breaking, transgress." Again let us go to Matthew 15:2-3:

"Why do Your disciples transgress (parabaino) *the tradition of the elders? For they do not wash their hands when they eat bread." He answered and said to them, "Why do you also transgress* (parabaino) *the commandment of God because of your tradition?"*

So to confirm what the meaning of this word "transgression" stands means, let us read from Acts 1:25:

To take part in this ministry and apostleship from which Judas by transgression (parabaino) *fell, that he might go to his own place.*

There is certainly a reason, why Matthew used five different words to describe and explain what sin is and what it does to us. Let us be aware and learn:

Translated Word	Greek Word	Meaning and Idea
DEBT	*opheilema*	**Something owed**
OFFENSE	*hamartia*	**To miss the mark** *(most common)*
TRESPASS	*parabtoma*	**Slide-slip, carelessness**
INIQUITY	*anomia*	**Conscious law breaking, lawlessness**
TRANSGRESSION	*parabaino*	**Intentionally breaking a command**

"Unrighteousness" and "unjust," are not translated by the word "sin," but instead by words like "iniquity," "wrong" and "injustice." For example, 1 John 5:17 says *All unrighteousness is sin* (hamartia)*, and there is sin* (hamartia) *not leading to death.*

THE DEBT OF OBEDIENCE

We must understand the difference between the five kinds of sin. God wants us to know this so the enemy does not have any stronghold in us, because he will trap us if we don't know what we are doing. We can now make sure that we will not fall back in to slavery under any of these five. We are constantly subjected or tempted in all these areas. We constantly need to come to our Father to repent and cleanse our self, and receive His forgiveness through the blood of Jesus.

We will realize more and more that sin is contrary to the holiness of God, that sin is a defilement, a dishonor, and a reproach to us, because it violates His command. Clearly it is a crime, and the guilt that comes to us when we sin then becomes a debt before God. We owe a debt of obedience unto our Maker and Governor. Because we have failed to render or pay our account of disobedience, we now have incurred a debt of punishment. The question becomes, how do we deal with that?

It is dealt with when we as Christians receive God's pardon through Jesus Christ. The Holy Spirit convinced us of our situation as sinners, we repented and received God's forgiveness and we were born again. We are being saved from eternal hell by His grace. Then why is it necessary to deal again with our sin or debt? It was paid once and for all on the cross. In Psalm 51:3 we can read:

> *For I acknowledge my transgressions,*
> *and my sin is **always** before me.*

There must be a very urgent reason to get our debt settled with God, because Jesus taught us to pray, *"Forgive us our **debts**."* The reason is because we keep on sinning. As the Holy Spirit

140

convinces us through the Word we become more aware of our sins, so we can repent and get rid of them.

As we recall, *since our severest problem is sin, our greatest need is forgiveness, and that is exactly what God provides*, but we must recognize our problem. Our accumulated sin becomes a mass of debt that has to be paid. So now let us find out through the Word of God how this can be done on a continuing basis and without guilt and condemnation. Romans 8:1 says,

There is therefore now no condemnation to those who are in Christ Jesus, who do not walk according to the flesh, but according to the Spirit.

"There is no condemnation," if we walk according to the Spirit, and consequently *there will be condemnation* if we do the opposite. It is not enough to be a born-again believer or to attend church every Sunday. It is *our daily living that will form our destiny*. There is no eternal salvation without eternal living. Here are some very good guidelines from Romans 8:13 and Galatians 6:8 and again in Romans 8:12:

*For if you live according to the flesh you will die; but if by the Spirit you **put to death** the deeds of the body, **you will live**.*

For he who sows to his flesh will of the flesh reap corruption, but he who sows to the Spirit will of the Spirit reap everlasting life.

*Therefore, brethren, **we are debtors**; not to the flesh, to live according to the flesh.*

Yes, we are debtors. To walk according to the Spirit, it will take works and deeds to produce the fruit of repentance. If for some reason we are not convinced about our eternal salvation through faith and works, maybe this from Titus 2:11-14 will help:

*For the grace of God that brings salvation has appeared to all men, teaching us that, **denying ungodliness and worldly***

lusts, we should live soberly, righteously, and godly in the present age, looking for the blessed hope and glorious appearing of our great God and Savior Jesus Christ, who gave Himself for us, that He might redeem us from every lawless deed and purify for Himself His own special people, zealous for good works.

And this is the way it works according to 1John 1:8-10:

1. *If we say that we have no sin, we deceive ourselves, and the truth is not in us.*

2. *If we confess our sins, He is faithful and just to forgive us our sins and to cleanse us from all unrighteousness.*

3. *If we say that we have not sinned, we make Him a liar, and His word is not in us.*

Three times the word "**if**" is used. The first and the last times tell us how we should not be and the middle one is the way it should work - notice, it says "*if we confess our sins.*"

OUR SIN IS ALWAYS BEFORE US

So sin, while it is once paid for and forgiven through Jesus Christ, it is still a reality in our daily life. Because we have found the Way does not mean that we can use another way. We constantly need the graciously offered forgiveness of our heavenly Father. When we walk in the Spirit we will be brought to the place of daily repentance.

Yes, we should sin less, and become more sensitive to the sin that stands in the way of our relationship with our Father and God. Yes, we should stop sinning and become holy like He is holy. Unconfessed sin can become like a barricade; and makes us hardened, impenitent and insensitive, following a life without joy and peace. Because we then miss that loving intimate fellowship with our Father and God, we are trapped in our unconfessed sin. We are blocked out, missing the mark and the result is that we can't offer the sacrifice of our lips. The our offering of praise and thanksgiving, the very reason that we were made. We end up losing that abundant life and the worst part is that we might lose our eternal life.

Like it says in 2 Corinthians 7:1, and Psalm 51:3 and 51:2:

*Beloved, **let us cleanse ourselves** from all filthiness of the flesh and spirit, perfecting holiness in the fear of God.*

For I acknowledge my transgressions,
and my sin is always before me.

Wash me thoroughly from my iniquity,
and cleanse me from my sin.

- *CONVICTION* **LEADS US TO CONFESSION**
- *CONFESSION* **BRINGS US TO REPENTANCE**
- *REPENTANCE* **CREATES NEW LIFE**
- **NEW LIFE OF** *FORGIVENESS,* **JOY AND PEACE**

This is the formula for *daily living* - not only once a week - to be reconciled through Jesus Christ to God our Father. Whoever confesses, repents and forsakes his sin will have mercy, because He is faithful and just to forgive us our sins and to cleanse us from all unrighteousness.

So when we have an unforgiving heart, when we carry grudges and harbor resentment, it might not seem to be a big sin, and it is not - merely a slide-slip - but we give Satan an advantage over us. The Holy Spirit cannot do anything else but lead us to repent and confess so that we will be forgiven, but if we just go on our life, if it be in ministry or not, we are unable to glorify our Father in heaven.

FORGIVE OUR DEBTORS

Forgiving others is the ultimate test. The principle is simple and clear- if we have forgiven, we will be forgiven - if we have NOT forgiven - we will NOT be forgiven. Forgiveness is the mark of a truly regenerate heart. We will display the victory and majesty of Jesus Christ when we forgive. Proverbs 19:11 and Psalm 66:19 each say:

The discretion of a man makes him slow to anger, and his glory is to overlook a transgression.

If I regard iniquity in my heart, the Lord will not hear.

When we quarrel because we are offended, or feel hurt because someone said the wrong word or they had a wrong attitude, is it a sin for us to react and quarrel? If we don't know let us look again at the word "transgression." The Hebrew word for transgression is *pesha* meaning "revolt, rebellion, sin, trespass, quarrel, and offend." The ancient Greek word *parabtoma* (a slide-slip) as we discovered earlier, means a more careless than intentional error, and it could be compared with the Hebrew word *pesha*. So the answer to that question is that we are not to react and get offensive and quarrel. That would be sin on our part. We are to overlook and forgive. Even if the other party is doing wrong it does not give us the right *to act in the natural and sin*, even though it is tempting. The fruit of the Spirit should be involved here and He wants us to be like His Son. Matthew 5:44-45 brings this point out even further as Jesus teaches us:

But I say to you, love your enemies, bless those who curse you, do good to those who hate you, and pray for those who spitefully use you and persecute you, that you may be sons of your Father in heaven.

The Apostle Paul warned us about this area in 2 Corinthians 2:10-11:

Now whom you forgive anything, I also forgive. For if indeed I have forgiven anything, I have forgiven that one for your sakes in the presence of Christ, lest Satan should take advantage of us; for we are not ignorant of his devices.

We see that Satan is the one to take advantage over us. When we have an unforgiving heart and when we carry grudges and harbor resentment, the Holy Spirit cannot work freely among us and we are unable to glorify our Father in heaven. This is one of Satan's devices, to keep us ignorant of what sin does to us. If we do not deal with it, we will suffer the consequences. In Matthew 5:23-24 Jesus reminds us of the urgency of this:

Therefore if you bring your gift to the altar, and there remember that your brother has something against you, leave your gift there before the altar, and go your way. First be reconciled to your brother, and then come and offer your gift.

When we think about it, we have a Father that is an author and expert on forgiveness, so we should take after Him. That is our ministry as it is explained in 2 Corinthians 5:18-19:

*Now all things are of God, who has reconciled us to Himself through Jesus Christ, and **has given us the ministry of reconciliation**, that is, that God was in Christ reconciling the world to Himself, not imputing their trespasses to them, and **has committed to us the word of reconciliation**.*

This is how we can go on in life missing God's mark for us, by neglecting to forgive each other and then we miss our calling so desperately. Ephesians 4:32-5:1 displays this truth:

*And be kind to one another, tenderhearted, forgiving one another, just as God in Christ forgave you. Therefore be **imitators of God** as dear children.*

To renew our mind in this area of forgiveness is to take on an attitude of Christ-like openness to one another, to give room for mistakes, to be alert and to not offend anyone. We should have a forgiving attitude and let go if we are offended, because we are to manifest a Christ-like character. Paul expressed this way in Ephesians 4:1-2:

*I, therefore, the prisoner of the Lord, beseech you to walk worthy of the calling with which you were called, with all lowliness and gentleness, with longsuffering, **bearing with one another in love**.*

It is so vitally important to understand how great God's forgiveness is and how we can activate and keep that unconditional love by imitating Him. We then see how He can forgive us and be so gracious toward us in spite of our continual trespasses. Through the Holy Spirit's leading we are able to do just that and then we understand why we need to forgive others. We need forgiveness in our life as an attitude. To take action as God's chosen people is an absolute condition. That is why Jesus deals with it again in Matthew 6:14-15 after He taught us how to pray:

For if you forgive men their trespasses, your heavenly Father will also forgive you. But if you do not forgive men their trespasses, neither will your Father forgive your trespasses.

So God deals with us just as we deal with others. When it comes to this matter we can certainly be sure of that. We are to forgive others as freely and graciously as God forgives us. Again in Matthew 18:21-35 Jesus bring this issue in the form of a parable, about "a certain king who wanted to settle accounts with his servants." We must read and learn that God means what He. The question is, do we act according to this? Or do we refuse and then suffer the consequences?

CLEANSING IN RELATION TO FORGIVENESS

To pursue this subject, we will look at both the Old Covenant and the New Covenant and how cleansing and the sprinkling of blood relate to this subject of forgiveness.

According to the Old Testament, when the people of Israel made a covenant or contract with God, in order to make it binding and legal it was done through sprinkling of blood. Let us read from Exodus 24:6-8:

And Moses took half the blood and put it in basins, and half the blood he sprinkled on the altar. Then he took the Book of the Covenant and read in the hearing of the people. And they said, "All that the LORD has said we will do, and be obedient." And Moses took the blood, sprinkled it on the people, and said, "This is the blood of the covenant which the LORD has made with you according to all these words."

They were now sanctified, cleansed, forgiven and fit to be in God's presence. As we go on reading from Exodus 24:9-11:

Then Moses went up, also Aaron, Nadab, and Abihu, and seventy of the elders of Israel, and they saw the God of Israel. And there was under His feet as it were a paved work of sapphire stone, and it was like the very heavens in its clarity. But on the nobles of the children of Israel He did not lay His hand. So they saw God, and they ate and drank.

That was an amazing event! Those men ate and drank in the very presence of God - what a fellowship and communion, whereas shortly before, they feared for their lives. Because the blood was sprinkled and they all understood the power, the forgiveness, and the safety that the cleansing blood brought, they did not fear anymore and their conscience did not hinder them anymore. What a glorious time it must have been!

As we continue to read from Exodus 12:21-25, we read the first Biblical reference to the sprinkling of the blood:

Then Moses called for all the elders of Israel and said to them, "Pick out and take lambs for yourselves according to your families, and kill the Passover lamb. And you shall take a bunch of hyssop, dip it in the blood that is in the basin, and strike the lintel and the two doorposts with the blood that is in the basin. And none of you shall go out of the door of his house until morning. For the LORD will pass through to strike the Egyptians; and when He sees the blood on the lintel and on the two doorposts, the LORD will pass over the door and not allow the destroyer to come into your houses to strike you. And you shall observe this thing as an ordinance for you and your sons forever. It will come to pass when you come to the land which the LORD will give you, just as He promised, that you shall keep this service."

We notice that as long as the blood was left in the basin, it had no effect; it was merely blood that had been shed. The blood had power to save only when it was lifted out of the basin and sprinkled according to God's instruction, "**strike the lintel and the two doorposts**."

This blood is a picture of the blood of Christ. If Christ is Lord in our life, then our doorposts - our hearts - are sprinkled by His blood, and we are clean, forgiven, constantly being renewed because He sprinkles the blood on our hearts in response to our faith. The blood of Jesus can not have the power in our lives if we are not being sprinkled by it. How clearly it is explained in Romans 3:25 and Hebrews 10:22:

Whom God set forth as a propitiation (a reconciliation) ***by His blood, through faith***, *to demonstrate His righteousness, because in His forbearance God had passed over the sins that were previously committed, let us draw near with a true heart in full assurance of faith, having our **hearts sprinkled** from an evil conscience and our bodies washed with pure water.*

As we noticed in Romans 3:25, "**God had passed over the sins that were previously committed**," so that is a Passover in the New Testament. When we are secure in the cleansing, forgiving, justifying, redemptive power of the blood of Jesus Christ, so that our conscience no longer condemns us, then we can rest assured that we have been sprinkled. Our conscience then stirs us to the obedience of the Word that was in the beginning - Jesus Christ. When the Holy Spirit is in command of our conscience and we act accordingly then we function properly. If the devil rises up with an evil accusation, our conscience proclaims the victory of the blood through our faith because our actions will follow our faith.

THE NEW COVENANT (AGREEMENT)

Let us follow how the New Covenant came in to being, by first reading from Jeremiah 31:31-32:

Behold, the days are coming, says the LORD, when I will make a new covenant with the house of Israel and with the house of Judah; not according to the covenant that I made with their fathers in the day that I took them by the hand to lead them out of the land of Egypt, My covenant which they broke, though I was a husband to them, says the LORD.

This is exactly what happened, and the prophecy is fulfilled. As we go on reading, the New Covenant or the Lord's Supper is instituted, which is the shedding of the blood of Jesus Christ, from Matthew 26:26-29:

*And as they were eating, Jesus took bread, blessed and broke it, and gave it to the disciples and said, "Take, eat; this is My body." Then He took the cup, and gave thanks, and gave it to them, saying, "Drink from it, all of you. **For this is My blood of the New Covenant**, which is shed for many for the remission of sins. But I say to you, I will not drink of this fruit of the vine from now on until that day when I drink it new with you in My Father's kingdom."*

We do notice the similarity, that again His people are sitting down at the table, fellowshipping and eating together with the Lord, just like Moses, Aaron, Nadab and Abihu were gathered with the 70 elders of Israel, when the first covenant was established. This Passover was planned ahead of time as shown in Luke 22:11, 22:15 and 22:20:

*Then you shall say to the master of the house, "The Teacher says to you, 'Where is the guest room where I may eat the **Passover** with My disciples?'"*

*Then He said to them, "With fervent desire I have desired to eat this **Passover** with you before I suffer."*

Likewise He also took the cup after supper, saying, "This cup is the new covenant in My blood, which is shed for you."

So let us conclude with understanding what the Lord's Supper means. The early church did it in order to remember the new covenant, as Jesus instituted and proclaimed this Passover celebration. Just as Passover celebrated deliverance from the slavery in Egypt, so the Lord's Supper celebrates deliverance and forgiveness from sin, because by Jesus Christ's death and the shedding of His blood we are being redeemed. God is passing our sins over. What more can we ask for when He makes us complete, as it so clearly states in Ephesians 1:7-12:

In Him we have redemption through His blood, the forgiveness of sins, according to the riches of His grace which He made to abound toward us in all wisdom and prudence, having made known to us the mystery of His will, according to His good pleasure which He purposed in Himself, that in the dispensation of the fullness of the times He might gather together in one all things in Christ, both which are in heaven and which are on earth; in Him. In Him also we have obtained an inheritance, being predestined according to the purpose of Him who works all things according to the counsel of His will, that we who first trusted in Christ should be to the praise of His glory

FORGIVE US OUR DEBTS AS WE FORGIVE OUR DEBTORS

Lessons in Prayer - Part Seven
"AND DO NOT LEAD US IN TO TEMPTATION BUT DELIVER US FROM THE EVIL ONE"

We now approach the part of the prayer that addresses temptation. Let us immediately pay attention to the translation of the word "temptation." Before we do that, let us prepare our minds using the words from Colossians 4:2

Continue earnestly in prayer, being vigilant (watchful, awake, active, and paying attention) *in it with thanksgiving.*

The word temptation refers to "inducement to evil, alluring, attractive, seductive, persuade, invite, provoke, or risk." The ancient Greek word *peirasmos* is translated in to English with the word 'temptation," but it is basically a neutral word in the ancient Greek language, having no necessary connotation either of good or evil. It has the idea of putting to proof by experiment (regarding good) or experience (regarding evil). So if we use the original Greek word in the text it will look like this; "And do not lead us in to testings, trials, examinations, do not try, discipline and assay us." That is the basic or the root meaning of the ancient Greek word *peirasmos* (temptation). It is by implication that we understand this to mean adversity, a condition of hardship or affliction. At the end of the definitions, the concordance implied the suggestion "temptation." The word "tempt" means, "to attempt, to persuade, to allure, to attract, seductively, provoking, inviting a person to do something evil or unwise."

When we look at all the words that define and explain the words "temptation" and "tempt," we do understand that God would never intend to tempt us in this sense. We can't even imagine that He would purposely induce us to commit sin. That is absurd, and James 1:13-14 explains it well:

*Let no one say when he is tempted, "I am tempted by God"; for God cannot be tempted by evil, **nor does He Himself tempt anyone**. But each one is tempted when he is drawn away by his own desires and enticed.*

God does not tempt anyone. So then why would we pray, "do not lead us into temptation"? A good suggestion here would be to replace the word "temptation" with the word "testing" and we would be more accurate. We can find the same word in James 1:2 and in James 1:3. They will explain it by using the word *testing* (the ancient Greek word *dokimion* which means, "approved, tried, trial, trying").

*My brethren, count it all joy when you fall into **various trials**, (peirasmos) knowing that the **testing** (dokimion) of your faith produces patience.*

It is not our intention to be involved in some debate on the work of translating the Bible. When several words can be used to express the meaning, sometimes they choose one word instead of another. It just will not justify the true meaning all the time so we will get some help by defining the words from the ancient Greek language, which is a very common practice in Bible study. Let us continue with 1 Corinthians 10:13:

*No **temptation** has overtaken you except such as is common to man; but God is faithful, who will not allow you to be **tempted** beyond what you are able, but with the **temptation** will also make the way of escape, that you may be able to bear it.*

As we are aware, the words "temptation" and "tempted" are here used, and in the ancient Greek, the word *peirasmos* is again used. Now however the translation "temptation" is more fitting than "testing" or "trials" and it does not contradict other

Scriptures. It may appear to be a difficult interpretative problem but we will be able to solve it, if we are aware and watch out.

These two lines that we are dealing with in the Lord's Prayer do reveal the heart of God's concern for us. Let us notice the difference. First, what does it mean if we are to say "and do not lead us in to temptation"?

We know that trials are a means for us to grow spiritually, morally, and emotionally; or to put it in another way, by various trials our character is strengthened. So then, are we to plead with our Father saying, "do not lead us in to trials"? It could be compared with a child that pleads with their parent saying, "We have a test in school. Do I have to go?" So we can see that this has nothing to do with temptation in its true meaning.

We should also consider the phrase, "But deliver us from the evil one." As the concordances define the word "temptation," we understand that it comes from the evil one or from ourselves. So this phrase has everything to do with attempts to persuade, to allure, to attract seductively, to provoke, inviting a person to do something evil or unwise. Temptation in itself is not a sin. It is rather the result when we yield to its inducements that lead us to sin and separation from our Father and God. We need desperately to be delivered from the evil one, so there is a plea to sustain us. There are two very different ways but still so related that our Lord Jesus teaches us on this point. Let us go to James 4:7-8 to get encouragement:

Therefore submit to God. **Resist the devil** *and he will flee from you.* **Draw near to God** *and He will draw near to you. Cleanse your hands, you sinners; and purify your hearts, you double-minded.*

What is Jesus actually teaching us, once we get the translation situation taken care of? When we obey and do God's will we don't face as many trials, testings, and examinations. Of course there are, we are always in the process of becoming more like Jesus. We stand in the need of Him to help us find the right way. But it is so vitally important that we separate what directly brings to us from the evil forces that attempt to destroy our faith and keep us seductively tempted. This is an issue that Jesus prayed about in His last prayer recorded in John 17:15:

I do not pray that You should take them out of the world, but that You should keep them from the evil one.

We can learn from Jesus. When He was tempted in the desert, He continued quoting Scripture, always answering temptation by saying, "IT IS WRITTEN." Jesus was able to resist all of the devil's temptation because He not only knew the Scripture, but He also lived and obeyed it. So knowing the Scripture is an unconditional step in helping us resist the devil's attacks, and we also have to obey and live accordingly. There are three crucial areas of temptation that the Devil focuses on:

- Wants and desires
- Possessions and power
- Pride and popularity

But Jesus did not give in to any of these temptations. Hebrews 4:15-16 says:

For we do not have a High Priest who cannot sympathize with our weaknesses, but was in all points tempted as we are, yet without sin. Let us therefore come boldly to the throne of grace, that we may obtain mercy and find grace to help in time of need.

There is much more that can be gained from continuing to study temptation and deliverance from the evil one. So please go on - pursue the riches of His Word and be in His will. Think again on this great final line in this wonderful prayer:

And do not lead us into testings, but deliver us from the evil one. For Yours is the kingdom and the power and the glory forever. Amen.

Let us receive through this prayer a revelation on how to pray found in Ephesians 1:17-19:

That the God of our Lord Jesus Christ, the Father of glory, may give to you the spirit of wisdom and revelation in the knowledge of Him, the eyes of your understanding being enlightened; that you may know what is the hope of His calling, what are the riches of the glory of His inheritance in the saints, and what is the exceeding greatness of His power toward us who believe, according to the working of His mighty power.

Nils-Erik Bergstrom welcomes your questions and comments. Nils is also available to speak to your Church or small group. You can contact him at

nils@enduringword.com

www.ingramcontent.com/pod-product-compliance
Lightning Source LLC
LaVergne TN
LVHW011202080426
835508LV00007B/545